CIVIL RIGHTS LEADERS

SINA DUBOVOY

Facts On File, Inc.

Civil Rights Leaders

Copyright ©1997 by Sina Dubovoy

Facts On File, Inc.
132 West 31st Street
New York NY 10001

Library of Congress Cataloging-in-Publication Data

Dubovoy, Sina.
    Civil rights leaders / Sina Dubovoy.
        p.   cm. — (American profiles)
    Includes bibliographical references and index.
    Summary: Profiles the lives and achievements of nine civil rights
leaders, including Ida B. Wells, A. Philip Randolph, Thurgood Marshall,
Rosa Parks, and Fannie Lou Hamer.
    ISBN 0-8160-3363-3
    1. Afro-American civil rights workers—Biography—Juvenile literature.
2. Afro-Americans—Civil rights—Juvenile literature. 3. Civil rights movements—
United States—History—Juvenile literature.   [1. Civil rights workers.   2. Afro-
Americans—Biography.]   I. Title.   II. Series: American profiles (Facts On File, Inc.)
E185.96.D83   1997
323.1'196073—dc20   96-2920

Facts On File books are available at special discounts when purchased in bulk quantities for businesses, associations, institutions or sales promotions. Please call our Special Sales Department in New York at 212/967-8800 or 800/322-8755.

Text design by Cathy Rincon
Cover design by Matt Galemmo

This book is printed on acid-free paper.

Printed in the United States of America

MP FOF 10 9 8 7 6 5 4

Contents

Introduction

The phrase *civil rights leaders* usually calls to mind the Revs. Martin Luther King, Jr., Jesse Jackson, and Andrew Young or Malcolm X and H. Rap Brown, all of whom were contemporaries in the 1960s. Many Americans are also under the impression that before Martin Luther King, Jr., there were no civil rights leaders of any real significance. And few people are aware that some civil rights activists were women.

One of the purposes of this book is to make readers understand that King and his contemporaries stood on the shoulders of giants, and that not all of these giants were men. Ida B. Wells and Mary Church Terrell, living in different regions of the United States, were part of a generation whose parents had been slaves. As the first generation of educated African-American women in U.S. history, they left an important legacy in their widely disseminated writings, in their lectures across the country and around the world, and in their social and educational activities. Long before Mohandas Gandhi of India became famous for his philosophy of public and political nonviolent resistance, these women were practicing it. And both women were charter members of the first civil rights organization for blacks, the National Association for the Advancement of Colored People, or NAACP, established in 1909.

Alabama-born and -raised, Rosa Parks will always be remembered for her famous bus ride that sparked King's civil rights movement. Her heroism did not begin and end with her refusal to yield her bus seat to a white man. Without her conscious participation in the year-long Montgomery bus boycott, which led to the loss of her job, her re-arrest, and threats against her life, the civil rights movement might not have been born there. Few realize that Parks might never have challenged the white establishment effectively without the civil rights training and education that she received as the legacy of some of the women and men presented in this book: Wells and Terrell and Frederick Douglass and William Monroe Trotter. Parks also was inspired by contemporaries such as Thurgood Marshall and A. Philip Randolph.

Martin Luther King, Jr.'s contributions are not diminished by the important strides made for African Americans by the civil rights leaders of earlier generations. No one was more aware of the accomplishments of those who came before him than was King, a man who sacrificed his own life for human rights.

Crusader for justice Fannie Lou Hamer, although a contemporary of King's, was part of the generation that took up the struggle after his untimely death. The civil rights movement from the time of Frederick Douglass onward was aimed at setting free such people as Fannie Lou Hamer—poor, uneducated, and living in the rural South. Ultimately, it was up to people like Hamer to bring the struggle home to their communities and neighborhoods, often block by block, street by street, and house by house. The reward for Hamer's enormous efforts seems small: securing the right of blacks to vote. Yet, her willingness to sacrifice her life and well-being toward this end makes her patriotism as great as that of any soldier on a battlefield.

Civil Right Leaders is not meant to be comprehensive; there were many people at the forefront of the civil rights struggle in America who are not included here. But we hope that the stories presented in this book will inspire readers to explore further the history of the civil rights movement and its other important figures. At the end of each chapter, a further reading list points readers to other sources of information on the subject.

The men and women depicted in the following pages were in most respects ordinary human beings. Yet they inspired many with their extraordinary spiritual courage and the strength of their convictions in the battle for social justice in the United States.

Frederick Douglass

FROM SLAVERY TO UNCERTAIN FREEDOM (C. 1817–1895)

One day in 1835, Frederick Douglass, a tall, young slave who had taught himself to read and write, had his fill of the landowner's, Edward Covey's, brutality. Young Frederick's owner had leased him out to Covey the year before to work his fields and perform other hard labor. During that time, "I was whipped, either with sticks or cowskins, every week," (Douglass 1994: p. 214, 221) and given little to eat. Finally Frederick decided to take matters into his own hands. "*I was resolved to fight*" (Douglass 1994: p. 242). When Covey started beating and kicking him in the stable one Sunday afternoon, Frederick hit back, to Covey's astonishment. Soon, the two were rolling in the dirt, kicking, cussing and struggling, yet "I was strictly on the *defensive*, preventing him from injuring me, rather than trying to injure him" (Douglass 1994: p. 242). When Covey cried out to

Opposite: *Frederick Douglass as he appeared in the 1840s, legally still a fugitive slave. He was an active abolitionist before the Civil War.* (Moorland-Spingarn Research Center, Howard University)

1

his other slaves for help, none came. The fight lasted a long time—until Covey gave up. Surprisingly, he let Frederick return to his farm work and never laid a hand on him again. Frederick from then on made up his mind to resist slavery with every fiber of his being, and to help his black brothers and sisters in the struggle for freedom.

Frederick Douglass knew little about his enslaved mother, Harriet, and nothing at all about his father, except that he was a white man. Harriet belonged to the lowest rung of the plantation slave hierarchy—the field hands. The women among them were often raped by their white owners and their sons or by the overseers. Working from dawn until dusk at hard physical labor in the master's fields, poorly clothed and poorly fed, Douglass' mother was outwardly no different from other slave women except, as Douglass later wrote, she was the only person of the 600 slaves on Colonel Edward Lloyd's plantation who could read. Douglass learned this fact after his mother's death.

He spent his first six years happily, living with his enslaved grandmother Betsey Bailey, her husband Isaac, a free black, and a slew of cousins. His grandmother's crude hut was located some distance from the Lloyd's big plantation house. There was almost no furniture and not a single bed, because slaves were expected to sleep on the floor and eat with their hands. Douglass grew up like other slave children, wearing only one long "tow linen" shirt both summer and winter, without shoes or undergarments. But Frederick was blissfully unaware that he was a slave, or that life would change for him after he turned six.

At that age, he was expected to join the many slaves who lived closer to the plantation owner's "great house," and to face whatever future his master had in store for him. The day arrived when his grandmother left him in the care of strangers—some of them his own brothers and sisters—whom he'd never met before, and he glimpsed with awe and fear a life he hadn't known existed.

The young boy learned quickly what it meant to be a slave. Outwardly, he looked and behaved like any other slave boy. However, Douglass' mind was keen, and from the beginning, his intellectual gifts set him apart from others and would later allow him to vividly recall and record his years of slavery, from 1824 to 1838.

As a child, he witnessed many beatings and whippings. Unseen one morning, the young Frederick witnessed Lloyd, the plantation owner, brutally whip a beautiful young slave woman. Douglass wrote: "He was cruelly deliberate, and protracted the torture, as one who was delighted with the scene" (Douglass 1994: p. 87). As a grown man, he, too, would be whipped.

Had it not been for the kindness of Lucretia Auld, the plantation manager's married daughter, the half-famished Douglass (whom she treated to snacks of bread and butter) might have led a life like his mother's or grandmother's. But because of Auld's influence, Douglass was sent to Baltimore. He was to live in the home of Hugh and Sophia Auld, Lucretia's relatives by marriage, as the companion of their son Tommy.

Douglass' seven year sojourn in Baltimore turned his life upside down. City living, even in a slave state, presented undreamed-of opportunities. However, Hugh Auld was furious when he learned that his wife was teaching Douglass to read the Bible. Of course, there was no stopping Douglass. Reading was opening his eyes to the fact that there were states where slavery did not exist, that there were people in these states, called "abolitionists," who said that slavery was evil and should be destroyed.

When Douglass was sent back to the Lloyd plantation, he was a changed person. His sole aim in life was to obtain his freedom. What lay ahead, however, were some of the worst years of his bondage. Meanwhile, Lucretia Auld had died of a fever. No one cared that for the first time in his life, Douglass would have to work as a common field slave.

His misery lasted three years. In that time, he would be "rented out" to various white farmers and beaten mercilessly. By then he had grown into a six-foot-tall, handsome young man. In his spare time, he organized Bible study groups and began plotting with other young slave men to escape to freedom. One such plot in 1836, with five friends who were also slaves, failed miserably when someone betrayed them. Lloyd, the plantation master, surprised Douglass by returning him to the Auld family, even promising to free him when he turned

25. Douglass figured that it was not kindness on Lloyd's part that motivated this decision, but simple common sense. An intelligent and literate slave like Douglass would find some way to escape, sooner or later.

Hugh Auld sent Douglass to work in the shipyards, where Douglass learned the caulker's trade of patching wooden ships. Soon he became the highest paid caulker. Working on the docks alongside free blacks was an education for him. The white caulkers treated both free blacks and slaves with contempt, even violence. Yet many of these same whites, like the plantation masters, were Christians who attended church every week. He could do nothing about such white hypocrisy, but he tried hard to change the attitude of the slaves. Many believed that God had willed their slavery and suffering and, therefore, they should endure them with meekness and humility. From his Bible readings, Douglass was certain that both blacks and whites, male and female, were equal in God's eyes—an unusual point of view for any black or white man in the 1830s.

Douglass continued spending his free time leading Bible classes, in which he also taught illiterate blacks the alphabet. At one of these classes, he met his future wife Anna Murray, who was five years his senior. She was a free black who would never learn to read and write, despite Douglass' best efforts.

In 1838, Douglass planned to escape and have Anna follow him later. He hopped on a train to New York City, disguised as a sailor. Once in New York, he happened to befriend a sailor who directed him to the home of black abolitionist David Ruggles. This was the first time in Douglass' life that he'd met an abolitionist. Because of the presence of Southern bounty hunters on the lookout for escaped slaves in New York, Ruggles advised Douglass to move on to New Bedford, Massachusetts. Few Southerners ventured into the most anti-slavery state in the nation. New Bedford also had shipyards, and Douglass could find work there.

He arrived in New Bedford in early September 1838; Anna Murray soon joined him, and they married immediately. A new life began for Douglass that was heady and exciting. It was his first taste of freedom. It didn't matter that the shipyards always turned him down for employment because he was black, even though work for ship caulkers was plentiful. Nor did it matter that his wife, like so many black women, was reduced to taking in other people's laundry for pitiful wages. Their wages were theirs to keep, and they were free to come and go as they pleased.

Douglass actually adopted his last name after his escape to freedom. Before that, he was known only as Frederick. Though he was now 20 and had never been to school, he learned from life itself. Moreover, he was highly literate and a voracious reader. He lacked only an outlet for his mental activity, which was not long in coming.

Although he'd been attending small antislavery rallies in New Bedford since his arrival, he now traveled for the first time to a major convention of the American Anti-Slavery Society, held in August 1841 in Nantucket. The famous abolitionist William Lloyd Garrison noticed Douglass and suddenly asked him to speak before the largely white audience. He was thunderstruck by their rapt attention and amazed at the overwhelming applause at the end. On the spot, the American Anti-Slavery Society hired him as a speaker and offered him a regular salary. His job was to relate to other audiences what he had so masterfully described that evening: the horrors of slavery, which he had experienced firsthand. He was a valuable addition to the antislavery cause in the North, because, while there were other black abolitionists, he was the only one who had escaped slavery and was still wanted for his "crime."

This marked the beginning of a lifelong, brilliant career for Frederick Douglass as a public speaker and as a powerful and effective writer. In the years between 1841 and the outbreak of the Civil War in 1861, Douglass emerged as a leading advocate of civil rights, not only for African Americans, but for all oppressed people, including women, who were denied the right to vote. The transition from abolitionist to civil rights leader was completed by 1860. In that year, in a speech at a Republican Party rally, he admonished voters to be mindful of "'the sacredness of human rights, the brotherhood of man'" (Huggins 1980: p. 69). Several years later, when slavery became illegal, he warned an audience that the struggle for emancipation was not over until all Americans, regardless of color, gender, or ethnic background, had equal rights.

Douglass' emergence as a leading civil rights spokesperson occurred slowly. Throughout the 1840s, as an important member of the American Anti-Slavery Society, he adhered strictly to the philosophy of its magnetic leader, William Lloyd Garrison. Garrison and others were convinced that the U.S. Constitution was a pro-slavery document and that the government was contaminated with the sin of slavery. Therefore, they believed abolition of slavery and equal rights for the freed slave had to be achieved through nonpolitical, "moral suasion," directed at slave owners. Hence, in his speeches and writings Douglass called on his listeners and readers to open their eyes to the sin of slavery and to God's wrath against slaveholders.

By the late 1840s, as editor of his own abolitionist newspaper, *North Star*, Douglass began resenting the attitudes of some well-meaning, white abolitionists. During his travels to Great Britain, from 1845 to 1847, he witnessed religious discrimination against Catholics, the denial of the vote to the poor, and the oppression of the Irish by their English overlords. This exposure to oppressed people elsewhere gave him a fresh perspective on American democracy. He began to appreciate the value of the U.S. Constitution, a document that few other countries had. Although its preamble did recognize the legality of slavery, he believed this could and would be changed. He also began to admire especially the Constitution's Bill of Rights.

By the 1850s, Douglass embarked on his own path, independent of Garrison and the American Anti-Slavery Society. He organized "Colored Men's Conventions" and rallied free blacks to do more, not only on behalf of slaves, but also for their entire race. While the *North Star* was primarily an abolitionist paper, the reader could find articles on many related subjects, from Irish independence to women's rights (throughout the 1850s, Douglass attended every women's rights convention). Always, the paper was laced with his controversial opinions.

Douglass even met and sympathized with the fiery abolitionist John Brown. However, he never could support Brown's violent tactics. When John Brown's raid of the federal arsenal in Harper's Ferry failed miserably on October 17, 1859, Douglass fled to Canada in fear that his name would be linked to Brown's. Luckily, it never was.

By the outbreak of the Civil War in 1861, Frederick Douglass was at the height of his mental powers and the most important African-American leader. Two dozen autobiographies by slaves were published in the North before the Civil War, but none were as widely publicized or read as Douglass' *Narrative of the Life of Frederick Douglass* and *My Bondage and My Freedom*. Kind English friends had sought out Douglass' former master, Hugh Auld, and purchased his freedom at last. Although he'd lived as a free man since his escape, he could have been captured and returned to slavery at any time. Now he was free of that fear.

Through his writing and editing of the *North Star*, Douglass reached a wide audience. In 1863, a year after Abraham Lincoln was inaugurated as president, he invited Douglass to the White House. This highest honor sent a clear message to Southern slaveowners. Although Douglass was deeply honored, he was then, as he would be two years later, unimpressed with the president.

Douglass felt that Lincoln was too slow in recognizing slavery as the central issue in the Civil War. Lincoln's Emancipation Proclamation of January 1863, which declared slavery illegal, seemed weak and timid. Douglass also was incensed that Lincoln, even as late as 1864, when the war was all but won, still favored the plan of deporting all African Americans back to Africa or to the West Indies, with money provided by Congress. Why not deport the Southern slaveholders instead, Douglass wondered? Finally, and most galling, was Lincoln's Reconstruction plan. This plan did not guarantee freed slaves their civil rights but heartily welcomed back the former rebels into the fold of the Union—if only 10 percent of a state's male population agreed to sign an oath promising to be loyal to the Constitution. More and more, Douglass sided with the radical Republicans in Congress who were staunch defenders of civil rights for African Americans—people such as Charles Sumner of Massachusetts and Thaddeus Stevens of Pennsylvania. These civil rights advocates in Congress believed that the federal government should use its power to uphold the rights of the freedmen.

While Douglass was critical of Lincoln, he was immensely saddened by Lincoln's assassination and feared that the new president, Andrew Johnson, onetime slaveowner from Tennessee, would be a lot worse. After President Johnson made the gesture of inviting Douglass to the White House—Douglass was anxious for his support of the African Americans' right to vote—Johnson listened politely. When Douglass left Johnson casually remarked, "'I know that damned Douglass; he's just like any nigger, and he would sooner cut a white man's throat as not'" (Huggins 1980: p. 113).

Douglass was aware, as were all African Americans, that a new phase in the struggle for the emancipation of blacks had started—a struggle that in some ways was far more frustrating than the fight against slavery. To be closer to Congress and the White House, Douglass moved his family to Washington, D.C., in 1872. The move came after an arsonist set fire to his home in Rochester, New York. Fortunately, his family got out in time and arrived safely in the nation's capital.

The Thirteenth Amendment (abolishing slavery) was passed in late 1865. Congress, overriding President Andrew Johnson's vetoes, passed the 14th Amendment in 1868, which guaranteed "equal protection of the laws" to all American citizens, including blacks. It also ushered into law the 15th Amendment in 1870, which granted men the right to vote regardless of "race, color, or previous condition of servitude." In 1875, Congress passed the Civil Rights Act so that there would be additional protection of the civil rights of African Americans. These were triumphant times for Douglass. From that moment on, he believed, the freed slaves and free blacks everywhere would be in control of their own destinies. These laws ended the arguments put forth by many whites to send blacks to Africa, or anywhere else. Douglass had always scorned opponents of full citizenship for blacks. "'Everyone in the country should be entitled to the same rights,'" he declared (Huggins 1980: p. 96). His faith in the Constitution was never stronger.

Yet full citizenship for women was a long way off. Douglass antagonized leading feminists, such as Elizabeth Cady Stanton and Susan B. Anthony, by insisting that black men's right to vote was more important at the moment than was women's. Douglass reasoned that at least the fathers, brothers, and husbands of white women had the vote, which was far more than African Americans had. The women did not support this argument, however, and friendship between Douglass and the women's rights activists cooled.

By now Douglass' friends were urging him to run for a political office, as a few other blacks were doing. Surprisingly, the man who'd campaigned tirelessly in every Republican election on behalf of civil rights for blacks was reluctant to become a politician. Douglass saw

A sketch of Frederick Douglass as he looked in his prime, shortly after the Civil War ended. (Library of Congress)

himself as an upper-class gentleman; as a world famous author, lecturer, and adviser of presidents. He'd been invited to become president of the newly chartered Freedman's Bank in 1873. The bank was meant to serve the financial needs of the newly freed slaves, who usually were hesitant or fearful of going into "white" banks. Douglass proudly and confidently accepted the position of president, but he soon realized that the bank was insolvent. When the bank closed its doors and many depositors were left without their hard earned savings, whites sneered at the incompetence of blacks, even though the bank's board of directors had been all white.

This failure did not diminish Douglass' popularity. Still, many younger blacks were becoming disillusioned with Douglass because his desire for a presidential appointment to some high public office was causing him to soften his stance toward the white establishment. Many viewed the Compromise of 1877, which removed all federal troops from Southern soil and returned the old planter aristocracy back into political power, as nothing short of a disaster. Soon one Southern state after another found ways to deprive African Americans of the right to vote. Northerners, who were growing tired of African Americans' seemingly endless plight, did nothing to intervene.

Douglass traveled throughout the South in 1888 and noticed the changes, the deterioration in race relations, and the loss of hope. By then, the U.S. Supreme Court had struck down the 1875 Civil Rights Act as unconstitutional. This decision became a green light to create segregation of hotels, restaurants, and other facilities. Segregation meant that blacks were excluded from "white only" buildings and other public areas.

Douglass joined a public protest against the Supreme Court decision. Younger blacks scoffed at him when he declared in public that some day the Court's decision would be reversed. Neither he nor his own children would live to see that happen, but he was right. Eighty years later his prediction came true.

Douglass' desire for a high government appointment was partially satisfied when he was named by President Ulysses S. Grant in 1871 to a temporary fact-finding mission to Santo Domingo. In 1889, Republican president Benjamin Harrison appointed him ambassador to Haiti, then the world's only black republic. He gladly accepted but resigned from this strenuous assignment less than two years later (he was in his seventies by then). Douglass also served as U.S. marshal for the District of Columbia and recorder of deeds. These appointments were far below his talents and expertise, but since no African American had ever held these positions, he accepted them gracefully.

Even in his old age, Douglass could still, now and then, show himself to be a warrior. Lynchings, or illegal hangings at the hands of a mob, had gotten so bad in the South that, together with a young black civil-rights leader, Mary Church Terrell, he visited the White House to plead for the president's help in securing a federal anti-lynching law. Unfortunately, they failed.

In the last decade of his life, segregation had swept through the public school system in the South. But Douglass never became bitter. He kept his faith in God and in the rule of law. He could never accept educator Booker T. Washington's point of view—that blacks should just work hard, "improve" themselves, and not "rock the boat" by demanding equal rights. Douglass believed in hard work—he was the very personification of the self-made man—but could never reconcile himself to inequality and segregation.

In his last years, he turned more and more inward. In 1878, he and his wife Anna had bought a hilltop mansion—which they called Cedar Hill—in the Anacostia district of Washington, D.C. Douglass took exceptional delight in his library and in the beautiful panorama of the city spread before him. If African Americans could not aspire to the presidency, Douglass at least had an unobstructed view clear down to the White House.

Anna died in 1882, and two years later, Douglass married Helen Pitts, a white suffragist (a feminist fighting for women's right to vote). The marriage shocked both black and white communities. Douglass pointed out that his first wife resembled his mother, while his second wife looked like his father. He didn't see what all the fuss was about. With his second wife Helen, Douglass invited many women's rights leaders and other famous people to their home.

After attending a women's rights rally on February 20, 1895, Douglass suddenly collapsed and died of a heart attack in his home. He was 77. His widow lived another eight years.

Even though Douglass was born and reared in servitude, denied the right to an elementary school education, and oppressed as a black man in a racist society, he could still say in his autobiography:

> Contemplating my life as a whole, I have to say that . . . my life has in many respects been remarkably full of sunshine and joy. While I cannot boast of having accomplished great things in the

Thirteen scenes depicting African-American history, published in 1897, a year after the Supreme Court legalized segregation. Frederick Douglass, top right, shown as an elderly statesman, was no longer living. (Library of Congress)

world, I cannot on the other hand feel that I have lived in vain (Douglass 1994: p. 619).

One might wonder what in fact Douglass did accomplish. The lives of most African Americans, even after emancipation, remained oppressed. Douglass watched in vain as white supremacists wrested precious, hard won civil rights from his black brothers and sisters in the years following the Civil War. He could do nothing to stop the tide of oppression against African Americans, even in the North. He achieved political appointments that few whites would have considered important. Yet his was a powerful voice on behalf of civil rights, a voice that even presidents listened to and respected. His journey from slavery to freedom, his concern for the oppressed throughout the world, inspired many. He was a visionary leader, the first in a long line of African Americans who were motivated by the spiritual ideals of brotherhood and equality.

Chronology

FEBRUARY 1817	Frederick Douglass born in Tuckahoe, Talbot County, Maryland
1818–1838	spends years in slavery
1838	escapes slavery; marries Anna Murray
1841	joins the antislavery movement as speaker and writer
1845	Douglass' first autobiography is published: *The Narrative of the Life of Frederick Douglass, an American Slave*
1845–1847	Douglass gives antislavery speeches throughout Great Britain
1847–1863	serves as editor of *North Star*
1848	attends first women's rights convention in Seneca Falls, New York

1855	Douglass' second autobiography published: *My Bondage and My Freedom*
1877–1881	Douglass serves as U.S. marshal for the District of Columbia
1881–1886	serves as recorder of deeds for the District of Columbia
1881	Douglass' third autobiography published: *Life and Times of Frederick Douglass*
1884	Douglass marries Helen Pitts
1889–1891	serves as ambassador to Haiti
FEBRUARY 20, 1895	Frederick Douglass dies in Washington, D.C.

Further Reading

Douglass' Works
Douglass, Frederick. *Autobiographies: Narrative of a Life, My Bondage & My Freedom, Life & Times.* Edited by Henry L. Gates, Jr. New York: Library of America, 1994. This volume contains all three biographies, up to 1881.

Books About Douglass
Huggins, N. I. *Slave and Citizen, the Life of Frederick Douglass.* Boston-Toronto: Little, Brown & Co., 1980. A short volume on the life of Douglass.

Keenan, Sheila. *Frederick Douglass: Portrait of a Freedom Fighter.* New York: Scholastic, 1995. A short book for young readers.

Kerby, Mona. *Frederick Douglass.* New York: Franklin Watts, 1994. An illustrated book for young readers.

McFeely, William S. *Frederick Douglass.* New York: Norton, 1991. A full and readable account of Douglass' life and struggles.

Patterson, Lillie. *Frederick Douglass: Freedom Fighter.* New York: Chelsea House, 1991. A full-length young adult biography.

Preston, Dickson J. *Young Frederick Douglass.* Centreville, Md.: Tidewater Publishers, 1980. Many new insights and facts about Frederick Douglass as a young slave.

Ida B. Wells

ANTILYNCHING CRUSADER AND AGITATOR FOR JUSTICE (1862–1931)

One afternoon in 1893, Frederick Douglass, who was well on in years, and his young friend Ida B. Wells were attending the World's Fair in Chicago. They decided to stop at a restaurant for a long lunch. As Wells describes in her autobiography, the city's Boston Oyster House was famous, and they both loved oysters. However, even in Chicago, "I understood that they did not serve colored people there." This aggravating fact merely goaded them to enter the restaurant, "cocked and primed for a fight if necessary. The waiters seemed paralyzed over our advent, and not one of them came forward to usher us to a table" (Wells 1970: p. 120). Nonetheless, Wells and Douglass proceeded to seat themselves at a table. Fortunately, the owner happened to be in that day, recognized Douglass, and greeted him cordially. Seeing this greeting, the waiters rushed to serve them, and they were able to eat their meal in peace. Douglass and Wells were lucky: the Supreme Court had declared the Civil Rights Act of

Ida B. Wells

"I'D RATHER GO DOWN IN HISTORY AS ONE LONE NEGRO WHO DARED TO TELL THE GOVERNMENT THAT IT HAD DONE A DASTARDLY THING THAN TO SAVE MY SKIN BY TAKING BACK WHAT I HAVE SAID." --1917

A youthful Ida B. Wells in 1917. By that time, the World War I years, the federal government had introduced segregation in its departments and would do nothing to pass a federal antilynching law. (Library of Congress)

1875 unconstitutional only a decade earlier. This meant that segregation was legal, and that eating in a restaurant—for an African American or anyone else not considered to be white—was a risk rather than a right. That day, Frederick Douglass, abolitionist and civil rights advocate, may have felt that he was passing the mantle of leadership to a younger generation of African Americans. Brilliant, fiery Ida B. Wells would not disappoint him.

Ida Bell Wells was born in Tippah County, Mississippi, into a slave family, on July 16, 1862. Her paternal grandfather was a white plantation owner who treated his illegitimate son Jim Wells comparatively well, but kept him in slavery. Jim Wells learned the carpenter's trade and later married another slave named Lizzie Warrenton, who was a talented cook. Together they had eight children; Ida was the oldest.

Wells was still a baby when the Civil War ended in 1865. After emancipation, her father stayed on the plantation as a carpenter, but as a free man working for wages. It was the era of Reconstruction in the South, and for the first time, all blacks had the right to vote. Some of them even ran for state and local offices, to most whites' horror. Too young to remember, Wells nonetheless heard the story of her father trying to exercise the right to vote: his boss fired him when he found out he'd voted the "wrong" ticket—Republican (the party of Abraham Lincoln) rather than Democratic (the party of Jefferson Davis, ex-president of the defeated Confederacy). Wells' father, who'd been saving up money, promptly opened his own carpenter's shop, which became a thriving business.

Wells' father was a good provider, and the family owned the home they lived in. Both parents impressed on their children the importance of getting an education. Wells' father could read and write, and eventually Wells' mother also became literate. "Our job was to go to school and learn all we could. . . . and my mother went along to school with us until she learned to read the Bible. After that she visited the school regularly to see how we were getting along" (Wells 1970: p. 9). In addition to keeping up in school, the young Wells was expected to care for the youngest children and see to it that they got their Saturday night bath.

Wells was deeply influenced by her parents' legacy of slavery, especially after hearing about the terrible experiences of her mother, who'd been cruelly beaten by her slave owners. She had been sold and resold at slave markets, until she lost all contact with her family. The evils of slavery and racial prejudice were imprinted on the girl's young mind and stayed with her the rest of her life.

Wells' religious upbringing also affected her profoundly. Her mother's piety set a powerful example. She recalled that her mother was "a deeply religious woman. She won the prize for regular attendance at Sunday school, taking the whole brood of six to nine o'clock Sunday school the year before she died" (Wells 1970: p. 9). Religious faith gave Wells the foundation on which she could fight against discrimination. She needed no further justification for her struggle for equal rights than the Golden Rule, to do unto others as you would have them do unto you. As a young woman, her first writings appeared in religious publications.

Wells' happy girlhood ended traumatically when her parents and one sibling died from yellow fever in 1878. She had just turned 16. The whole community of tiny Holly Springs, Mississippi, where the family lived, was astonished at Wells' stubborn determination to care for her remaining five brothers and sisters on her own (another sibling had died some years earlier). Within a few short months of her parents' death, she'd passed the country schoolteacher's exam and landed a job as a grade-school teacher in a one-room schoolhouse six miles outside of town.

It was hard work. She trekked to and from her school on a mule; every weekend she spent washing, ironing, and cooking for the rest of the week. Her leisure activity was reading, and that she did voraciously—Charles Dickens, Emily and Charlotte Brontë, and Louisa May Alcott. "I had read the Bible and Shakespeare through, but I had never read a Negro book or anything about Negroes," (Wells 1970: pp. 22–23) even though she lived in a state where the majority of the population was black. There were very few published books by black authors at this time. She developed a taste and an appreciation for the written word and for good literature.

When she was 21, Ida moved to Memphis, Tennessee, where there were more opportunities. Relatives helped care for her sisters, and her brothers were earning their own living as apprentices. While living in Memphis and teaching at the same country school, she studied for the city teacher's exam, hoping to earn a larger salary.

One May day in 1884, while riding the train from Memphis back to her teaching job in the country, an event occurred that changed the course of her life. Only the previous year the Civil Rights Act of 1875 (in which the federal government made it illegal for any private person or proprietor to practice discrimination in housing, public facilities, and so forth) was declared unconstitutional. Now it was up to the states to protect the rights of their black citizens. They responded—one Southern State after another—by passing "Jim Crow" laws that interfered with black men's right to vote and sanctioned segregation, the separation of the races. Booker T. Washington—a prominent African-American spokesperson in the South and a successful, self-made man and former slave—counseled blacks to tolerate discrimination and concentrate instead on "improving" themselves. Frederick Douglass disagreed but could only advise "patience."

Ida Wells rode the train that afternoon immersed in her own thoughts about the impending city teacher's exam and her new life in Memphis. The train conductor, coming by to take tickets, suddenly ordered her out of the train car and into the car reserved for "coloreds." When she refused to budge, he yanked her out of the compartment by force while white passengers cheered and jeered. Rather than sit in the segregated train car, she got off at the next stop; her rage and humiliation were all that she could remember afterward.

Wells returned to Memphis and, incredible for a woman in that day and age, hired a lawyer to sue the railroad company. Surprisingly, she won her case, and the railroad company was forced to pay her a handsome fine of $500. But Wells knew she'd been lucky; the judge happened to be a transplanted Northerner who'd fought on the Union side in the Civil War.

Up until then, Ida had never been concerned with anyone's problems except her own. That attitude was altered forever. Not long after the incident, she wrote a detailed description of her experience with racism for her Baptist church weekly, *The Living Way*, and signed it with the pen name "Iola." Her article attracted such favorable attention that the pastor asked her to write for the magazine regularly. From then on, the written word became an important medium for her strong and often controversial opinions.

Her fellow African Americans—who stood to gain in her triumph against the railroad—did not offer much support, however. "None of my people had ever seemed to feel that it was a race matter and that they should help me with the fight" (Wells 1970: p. 21). The lack of aid from other black Americans was a problem that would haunt her for the rest of her active career.

African-American publications throughout the country began re-printing her articles from *The Living Way*, even requesting her to write for them. By then, she was a schoolteacher in the segregated Memphis school system and became active in a literary club made up largely of black teachers. The requirement that members engage in debates and deliver "recitations" was actually preparing Wells for her future as a public speaker. Wells' literary activities and constant reading closed the gap left by her unfinished education.

Already in her mid-twenties, independent and resourceful Wells was clearly in danger of becoming what people commonly called an "old maid." The attractive Memphis schoolteacher had plenty of young men courting her. A few even proposed marriage. "'I feel so disappointed in them all,'" she wrote sadly in her diary (Thompson 1990: p. 18). She resigned herself to remaining single for life and dedicating herself to the cause of racial justice.

As a writer for the American Baptist Press, she attended her first African-American press convention in 1886. Three years later, she went to the Colored Press Association's Convention in Washington, D.C. This convention was a thrilling experience for her. She was the only woman journalist attending, and she had never been East in her life. There she met Frederick Douglass, who was already a very famous man, for the first time. This was the beginning of a friendship that ended only with his death, six years later.

By 1890, Wells was becoming tired of teaching, which she had been doing since the age of 16. She was not very popular with the other teachers and felt she had little in common with them. One day in 1891, when fellow teachers read a scathing article of hers criticizing the conditions of the black public schools and the incompetence of most of the teaching staff, Wells lost her job. She had been trying to draw attention to the poor quality of black schools compared with white schools, but instead of appreciating her intention, the black teachers in Memphis took her criticisms personally. Wells was especially dismayed at the attitude of the parents of the children she had been trying to help, who "couldn't understand why one would risk a good job, even for their children!" (Wells 1970: p. 37).

Losing her job in 1891 gave Wells the courage to devote herself full-time to writing. Two years earlier, she'd once again done the unconventional, buying a partnership in the African-American newspaper, *Free Speech*. This partnership was shared equally with two men. One partner, the Reverend Nightingale, had founded the paper in his Beale Street Church. Wells now began writing freely on topics of her choosing. She exposed the evils of segregation and the suppression of black civil rights. Another favorite target of her criticism was the submissiveness of blacks to injustice, which she hated as much as white violence. "'The more the Afro-American yields and cringes and begs . . . the more he is insulted, outraged and lynched'" (Townes 1993: p. 126), she stated in her usual direct manner.

Wells' provocative opinions soon made *Free Speech* the most popular black publication in the South, its readership climbing from 1,500 to 4,000 in less than a year. Even Southern white newspapers occasionally noticed her writing, which they cited as examples of black "arrogance." Black publications as far away as New York often quoted her articles and cited her opinions. As the only black woman editor in the country, and one of a handful of women editors, she was a celebrity. "'Somebody must show that the Afro-American race is more sinned against than sinning, and it seems to have fallen upon me to do so'" (Thompson 1990: p. 30). As a full-time editor and writer, Ida had at last found her true vocation.

She loved her life in Memphis. While outrages against blacks occurred throughout the South (the number of lynchings of blacks averaged 150 per year throughout the 1880s), they always seemed to be happening somewhere else. For that reason, everyone, including Wells, was caught off guard when ugly racial violence surfaced in Memphis on a spring day in March 1892: The husband of Wells'

1. T. Thomas Fortune, Journalist.   2. Booker T. Washington, Educator.
3. Hon. Frederick Douglass, Statesman.
4. I. Garland Penn, Author, Orator;   5. Miss Ida B. Wells,
Chief Commissioner, Atlanta Exposition.   Lecturer, Defender of the Race.

Wells was the only African-American woman to have her photograph placed along with prominent black leaders and opinion makers. The young Wells, in this 1890s photo, was at the height of her career as a journalist, lecturer, and agitator. (Moorland-Spingarn Research Center, Howard University) best friend in Memphis and two other black men were brutally murdered in broad daylight by a mob of whites. Thomas Moss was only in his twenties, and his wife was pregnant with their second child.

Wells was in Natchez, Mississippi, when the incident occurred; afterward, she reported what she'd learned firsthand about the murders in *Free Speech*. This time, the lynching was not for alleged rape, which was the favorite excuse for killing blacks. Thomas Moss, gunned down in his own grocery store along with his two partners, was taking away too much business from the white store owner in the same neighborhood. After the lynchings, Moss' store was heavily damaged and eventually closed when creditors withdrew their financial support. There was no restitution for damages and no arrest of the perpetrators of the horrendous crime. In fact, some considered that Thomas Moss was "lucky." A year later, in Paris, Texas, a black man accused of rape was tortured and burned alive before jeering spectators, including children.

Ida was at her fiery best when exposing the truth. She ignored the consequences to herself in writing about the incident. Her article attracted wide attention even in the white press. While her friends urged her to back off for fear of reprisals against her, she answered them by buying a pistol: "I felt that one had better die fighting against injustice than to die like a dog or a rat in a trap" (Wells 1970: p. 62), she wrote. She continued her agitation by supporting economic boycotts against whites and emigration of blacks from Memphis to the freer land of Oklahoma, newly opened for settlement. An exodus began at her urging, to the dismay of white businessmen; the streetcar company in Memphis appealed personally to Wells to use her influence to get blacks riding the streetcars again. While the uproar surrounding the lynchings eventually died down, Wells proved how one person can make a difference.

Whites accused her of inciting violence while they did nothing at all to stem their own racial hatred. In fact, while Wells was away on a speaking trip in May 1892, a furious white mob broke into the *Free Speech* office and "ran the business manager, J. L. Fleming, out of town, destroyed the type and furnishings of the office, and left a note saying that anyone trying to publish the paper again would be punished with death" (Wells 1970: pp. 61–62). This incident put

Wells on notice not to return to Memphis. In New York City, the editor of the prestigious African-American newspaper *New York Age* offered her a job at once. She gratefully accepted and never returned to Memphis.

Ida B. Wells' agitation began to attract the attention of British liberal reformers. In 1893, she accepted an invitation for a long stay in Great Britain to educate white audiences there about the ill treatment of blacks in America. That same year, she had accepted a job as editor of the *Chicago Conservator*, deciding to make Chicago, rather than New York, her home base.

Although Great Britain was the largest colonial power in the world, and, thus, the oppressor of many people of color, Wells encountered only kindness while she was there. For the first time in her life, she lived with white people in their homes. Wells found that middle-class English women were less inhibited than their American counterparts. Years later, she vividly recalled her shock at the sight of "decent" women reaching for their cigarettes after dinner.

Wells hoped that well-connected, influential white people in England and Scotland could pressure white Americans to put a stop to the lynchings of black Americans. By the time she returned from her second trip to Great Britain as a guest of British religious and reform groups, an Anti-Lynching Committee had been established in London, and their letters to the governors of Southern states were effective, even though they enraged some politicians. The governor of South Carolina said that any sheriff in the state who failed to protect any person suspected of a crime would lose his job. Between 1893 and 1897, one Southern state legislature after another passed antilynching laws. Prominent Northern whites, such as the "Uncrowned Queen of America," Frances Willard, who headed the 200,000-member Women's Christian Temperance Union, denounced lynching, as did labor leader Samuel Gompers and influential Northern editors.

When she returned from her second trip to Great Britain in July 1894, Wells was greeted in New York Harbor like a conquering hero. But Wells refused to let up on the struggle. Instead, she took a leave of absence from her new Chicago job to undertake a grueling, coast-to-coast tour to bring her campaign against lynching to the

American public. Frederick Douglass became her unabashed admirer and enthusiastic supporter. Nonetheless, many of her fellow African Americans, especially the educated, did not share Douglass' enthusiasm. A former business associate of hers even wrote that "'her fire eating speeches nowhere in the globe will help the situation'" (Townes 1993: p. 158). Ambivalent support from her own race frustrated her time and again. Exhausted after her year-long crusade, she settled down to her editorial job in Chicago.

The Chicago Conservator, the nation's oldest African-American newspaper, was owned by a respected lawyer, Ferdinand L. Barnett. From the time that he coauthored an 81-page booklet with Wells in 1893—"The Reason Why the Colored American Is Not in the World's Fair"—he'd fallen head over heels in love with her. At first it was a one-sided attraction. Ida was 30 when she met him, too "old" and far too dedicated to think of marriage. But Ferdinand Barnett persisted for two years. In the end, he won her over. She had never met any man as kind and gentle as he, a widower with two young children. For his part, he knew he would never meet another woman as courageous and unconventional as Wells. Several months after their wedding in Chicago in 1895, the new Mrs. Barnett was shocked to learn that, at age 33, she was expecting a child. A year later, she packed up baby Charles and, together with a nanny, headed alone for the East Coast to go on a whirlwind lecture tour.

The cause of civil rights would take a backseat to motherhood as long as Wells' children were small. Nonetheless, she accomplished a great deal for the cause while raising four rambunctious youngsters. Throughout these years, she continued to be active in the black women's club movement, which she'd helped found in the mid-1890s. She also enjoyed teaching a young men's Bible class every Sunday. Many of these young men became professionals, some even running for political office. She hoped to influence them to apply spiritual principles to all of their activities, private as well as public.

In 1908, 13 years after her marriage and while her children were still very young, Ida B. Wells established the Negro Fellowship League on State Street in Chicago, modeled after the Young Men's Christian Association (YMCA), with the financial help of a concerned white woman, Mrs. Victor Lawson. Wife of the *Chicago Daily*

News editor, Mrs. Lawson was appalled when she learned that Chicago's large, well-endowed YMCA excluded blacks. Eventually Wells funded the project out of her own income, which she earned as Chicago's first African American, and first woman, adult probation officer.

In 1909, Ida B. Wells became one of the founding members of the National Association for the Advancement of Colored People (NAACP). She was one of its representatives in 1913 when, together with black militant William Monroe Trotter, she met with newly elected President Woodrow Wilson to protest his introduction of segregation into the federal government, the only woman in the black delegation.

When the state of Illinois permitted women to vote in 1914, Wells organized the Alpha Suffrage Club, which sent women to all the voting districts in Chicago to register black women voters. Frequently black men jeered at the long-skirted women tramping door-to-door to get the women's vote. Wells instructed her suffragists to tell such men that they were helping black men get elected. When a white candidate running for mayor of the city in 1915 asked "who the masses of colored people accepted as leader . . . he found that it was not a man but a woman, and that I was that woman," noted Wells in her memoirs (Wells 1970: p. 349).

In 1930, a year before her death, Wells ran for an Illinois state senate seat, which she lost to her black male opponent. Nonetheless, she set a powerful example for other African-American women to follow.

Toward the end of her active and dedicated life, she began writing her memoirs. Sudden illness and her untimely death in 1931 prevented her from turning her autobiography into a published book. *Crusade for Justice, the Autobiography of Ida B. Wells* was finally published in 1970, years after her death. It is lucid, powerful writing from the pen of a seasoned journalist, editor, and activist.

In late March 1931, Ida B. Wells suffered a sudden onset of uremia poisoning (kidney failure). A few days later, on March 25, she died in a Chicago hospital at age 68.

All her life Wells encountered black men and women who threw up their hands in despair, declaring that nothing could be done about the injustices that they suffered. Yet Ida B. Wells was born of parents who'd been slaves; she'd grown up in an era when women were expected to be weak, helpless, and dependent; she was without professional opportunities; and she lacked the benefit of a higher education. Her parents died when she was a young girl, leaving her to care for her siblings. In addition to these disadvantages, she was a member of a despised minority. Despite these impediments, she became a very prominent American woman, the first African-American female journalist, editor, and publisher of her own newspaper, and a much-sought-after public speaker in the United States and Great Britain.

Education and religious faith were the bedrock of her life and character. Without them, it would be difficult to imagine Ida B. Wells. Education—in her case, self-education—began early and became a lifelong pursuit. Religion gave her the strength, hope, and perseverance that sustained her through bitter disappointments, as well as a vision of justice. By her actions and example, Ida B. Wells adhered to the same high standards of nonviolence and faith that Frederick Douglass, her friend and mentor, had followed, and she carried on his spiritual and moral crusade.

Chronology

JULY 16, 1862	Ida B. Wells is born in Holly Springs, Tippah County, Mississippi
1878	Parents and sibling die of yellow fever; Wells starts teaching career and providing for the family.
1884	is thrown out of railroad car for "whites only"
1891	begins full-time career as editor and writer for *Free Speech*
1892	Close friend Thomas Moss brutally lynched in Memphis; Wells begins crusade against lynching
1893–1894	makes antilynching speeches in Great Britain (two trips); forms Anti-Lynching Committee

1893	publishes "The Reason Why the Colored American Is Not at the World's Fair"
1894–1895	embarks on a coast-to-coast antilynching crusade
1895	publishes "A Red Record: Tabulated Statistics and Alleged Causes of Lynchings in the United States, 1892–1893–1894"
1909	is one of the founding members of NAACP
1910	establishes Negro Fellowship League
1913	is the only woman in delegation to White House to protest segregation in federal government
1914	Establishes women's Alpha Suffrage Club
1928	begins writing her autobiography (published after her death)
1930	serves as candidate for Illinois state senate seat
MARCH 25, 1931	Ida B. Wells dies of kidney failure, Chicago

Further Reading

Books By Ida B. Wells

Wells, Ida B. *Crusade for Justice: The Autobiography of Ida B. Wells.* Edited by Alfreda M. Duster. Chicago: University of Chicago Press, 1970. This provides a wonderful, page-turning account of Wells' life.

———. *Selected Works of Ida B. Wells-Barnett.* New York: Oxford University Press, 1991. Contains her best known writings on lynching and on the exclusion of African Americans from the Chicago World's Fair.

Books About Ida B. Wells

Klots, Stephen. *Ida Wells-Barnett.* New York: Chelsea House Publishers, 1994. This concise illustrated biography for young readers contains an extensive bibliography.

Sterling, Dorothy. *Black Foremothers: Three Lives.* Old Westbury, N.Y.: Feminist Press, 1979. Short, easy-to-read, illustrated account of Ida B. Wells' life. Also includes the lives of Ellen Craft and Mary Church Terrell.

Thompson, Mildred I. *Ida B. Wells Barnett: An Exploratory Study of an American Black Woman, 1893–1930.* Brooklyn, N.Y.: Carlson Publishing, Inc., 1990. Next to her autobiography, this is the most comprehensive book on Ida B. Wells' life.

Townes, Emile M. *Womanist Justice: Womanist Hope.* Atlanta, Ga.: Scholar's Press, 1993. A religious and spiritual perspective of Ida B. Wells.

Mary Church Terrell

INTEGRATIONIST (1863–1954)

Traveling in Europe as a young woman in the 1880s, Mary Church stayed for some weeks at the home of a German family, eager to learn the language firsthand. Germans seemed to her to be color blind, until one day she discovered another form of race hatred:

> I enjoyed the mischief and fun of the younger daughter, but the bond of union between us would have been much closer if she had not hated the Jews so fiercely and bitterly. It amazed me to see how a girl so young could hate so deeply a race, no representative of which had ever done either her or any member of her family any harm (Terrell 1940: p. 89).

Opposite: *Mary Church in 1884, as a young graduate of Oberlin College, the second African-American woman in U.S. history to obtain a college degree. (The first was Mary Jane Patterson, who graduated from Oberlin in 1862.)* (Moorland-Spingarn Research Center, Howard University)

This experience opened her eyes to the mistreatment of minorities around the world, and she realized that black Americans were one of many oppressed groups. For the rest of her life, Terrell was sensitive to the plight of minorities everywhere, as well as women.

At her birth on September 23, 1863, no one would have dreamed that she would become a leader of her race, a champion of women's rights, and one of the most educated African-American women of her generation. "A white woman has only one handicap to overcome—that of sex. I have two—both sex and race," begins the story of Mary Church Terrell's life, which she wrote in her seventies, when her biggest civil rights battles still lay ahead (Terrell 1940: p. 1).

Terrell was born the year that Lincoln issued the Emancipation Proclamation, which freed the slaves in the Confederate states. But Terrell's parents remained slaves, since the family lived in Tennessee, a slave state that remained loyal to the Union. The nationwide end of slavery would not come until 1865 and the passage of the 13th Amendment. Still, Terrell had no personal experience of slavery or, for that matter, poverty, thanks to her remarkable parents. When all slaves were freed after the Civil War, both her father and mother became extremely successful in business. Her mother Louisa Ayers' hair-dressing salon in Memphis was so profitable that "It was she who bought the first home and the first carriage we had" (Terrell 1940: p. 9). Her father, Robert Church, son of a white slave owner, had never gone to school but had managed to teach himself to read. As a saloon keeper in Memphis after the Civil War, then as a hotel owner, and eventually, as a banker and Memphis' wealthiest businessman, Robert Church demonstrated his flair for making money. Terrell's parents had been treated relatively well by their slave owners. Hence, what Terrell came to know about the horrors of slavery she absorbed from her grandmother, "who told me tales of brutality perpetrated upon slaves who belonged to cruel masters," the lot of many slaves, including her grandmother (Terrell 1940: p. 11).

Terrell grew up in a well-to-do and sheltered family environment. Even though her father had been brutally assaulted in an ugly racial incident after the Civil War, he discouraged any discussion of racism with his daughter Mary and her brother Thomas. Unlike other famous civil rights leaders such as Douglass, Wells, and Trotter, Terrell was shielded as much as possible from the problems of her race. That such a pampered child "dreamed of the day when I could promote the welfare of my race" (Terrell 1940: p. 60), seemed quite unlikely.

Terrell's journey toward racial consciousness and pride began early. First, there were her grandmother's stories about slavery. Then she experienced her own near expulsion from a "whites only" train car at the age of five because the conductor discovered that she was black. Most important, she was influenced by her education, which led her on a journey to self-discovery and self-awareness.

Terrell's mother and father, who had separated and divorced in 1869 when she was only six ("this pained and embarrassed me very much" [Terrell 1940: p. 10], refused to send her to the inferior black public schools of Memphis. Instead, she began her education in Yellow Springs, Ohio, at the expensive, progressive "model school" attached to Antioch College. This school accepted children of all races. Terrell loved learning, and with parents who spared no expense for her schooling, she obtained the best education possible for an American woman—white or black—in that day and age.

She graduated from Oberlin High School in Oberlin, Ohio, in 1880 and planned to enroll in the difficult, four-year classical program at Oberlin College, which few women before her had attempted. Female students almost always settled for the easier, two-year certificate program, which did not require fluency in Greek and Latin. Terrell's friends warned her against choosing the four-year "gentlemen's course," since it would ruin her chances of finding a husband. Because she did want to marry and raise a family some day, she agonized over her decision. Terrell turned to her father for advice. To him the decision was very simple: "I might remain in college as long as I wished and he would foot the bill" (Terrell 1940: p. 32).

Terrell never regretted her decision to stay at Oberlin College for four long years, which turned out to be among the happiest of her life. She excelled in languages, and Greek became her favorite subject. She became class poet, editor of the *Oberlin Review*, and joined the literary Aeolian Club; she learned to speak in public and conduct meetings. These invaluable experiences prepared her for her future role as a civil rights leader.

Terrell knew that, as an African-American woman in college less than 20 years after slaves had been freed, she was a trailblazer. Despite the fact that she was immersed in white culture, she maintained her identity as an African American. And her history classes taught her an extremely important lesson—that "no race has lived upon the face of this earth which has not at some time in its history been the subject of a stronger race. This fact . . . greatly increased my self-respect" (Terrell 1940: p. 21).

If her sense of history gave her understanding, her Christian faith gave her hope. Many black intellectuals of her generation rejected religion because of the church's failure to speak out against segregation and racism. But Terrell made a distinction between the church, which imperfect human beings organized and ran, and religion, which came directly from God.

Photographs of Terrell in her high school and college years reveal a pretty girl of medium height, light-complexioned, and always stylishly dressed. She loved to dress well all her life, but even more than that, she loved to dance and laugh, even into old age.

In 1884, Terrell graduated from Oberlin College with many honors. Now that her formal schooling was over, she wanted to use her education to earn a living. In this aim she collided head on with her father, a conservative Southerner at heart, who would not hear of a daughter of his actually *working* for a living. As a divorced man living alone in a big house in Memphis, he insisted that she live with him until she married. But when nonsegregated Wilberforce University in Ohio offered her a teaching position, she couldn't resist the offer. She packed her bags and set off, and her disgruntled father reconciled himself to having a daughter with a mind of her own.

In 1885 segregation was becoming a strong force in the South, and racism was increasing in the North. Wilberforce University seemed remote from these harsh realities, a haven of reason and security. Terrell was 22 years old and had experienced only interracial harmony and integration in her long years of private schooling. Wealthy and sheltered though she was, Terrell had no illusions about the real world outside the ivy-covered walls of academia. For example, in seeking a summer job as a college student in New York City (where her divorced mother lived), Terrell had experienced discrimination. Despite her numerous attempts to get hired for the few jobs deemed suitable for women in those days, she was always turned down the moment she met a prospective employer face to face.

Though Terrell was happy teaching at Wilberforce, she didn't think twice about leaving Ohio when she received a job offer to teach at M Street High School in Washington, D.C. M Street was an all-black school in an increasingly segregated city. She knew that, as one of only a handful of college-educated African-American women, she would be an important role model, especially for black girls.

At M Street High School (which later became Dunbar High School, in honor of the black poet Paul Dunbar) during the fall of 1886, Terrell taught French and Latin. Although it was a black high school, the curriculum as well as the teachers reflected a strong identification with white European culture. There was little interest in African-American studies and none at all in African languages.

Although Terrell strove all her life to instill a sense of racial pride in fellow African Americans, she too was steeped in European culture and values. At that time in American history, it seemed more urgent for black Americans to assimilate into the dominant culture, which identified itself most closely with its Northern European origins. Acceptance of blacks and other minorities by the dominant culture would be more assured if they could blend in with the mainstream and accept its values. It's important to remember that American "unity in diversity" and the promotion of multiculturalism is a relatively new idea.

A year after Terrell began teaching at M Street High School, she took a leave of absence and set off to Europe on a luxury ocean liner with her father in 1887. He stayed with her for only a short time. It was also his very first trip abroad.

Terrell ended up spending two years in Europe. She greatly enjoyed the beauty of the places she visited and the sophistication of the Europeans; as she rapidly absorbed French and German. She loved the orderliness, cleanliness, and high level of culture in Germany, but the widespread anti-Semitism (prejudice against Jews) that she encountered repelled her. She liked France even better. In that country, dark-skinned people seemed to be welcome and treated with respect. In Berlin, Germany's capital, she had been pressured to move out of her boarding house when two white American medical students from the South moved in and complained about Terrell's presence. They explained to the astonished landlady that "Just as Jews are socially ostracized in Germany, so Negroes are socially ostracized all over the U.S." (Terrell 1940: p. 86). The woman related this conversation to Terrell.

Still, Terrell continued to admire Germany and felt that not all Germans were blinded by racism. A young German even proposed marriage to Terrell. She turned him down, although the attraction was mutual. An unexpected consequence of Terrell's European sojourn was her discovery of her American identity. She realized that to remain in Europe would be to opt for an easy course in life. "I knew I would be much happier trying to promote the welfare of my race in my native land, working under hard conditions" (Terrell 1940: p. 99).

A much wiser, more sophisticated young woman returned home and resumed her teaching position at M Street High School in 1889, but not for long. She fell deeply in love with a handsome Latin teacher, Robert Terrell. He was a Harvard graduate with a law degree from Howard University. Soon he would become the first federally appointed African-American judge in U.S. history. Moreover, he was a firm believer in women's rights and a woman's right to vote.

After their marriage in the fall of 1890, Terrell had to give up her teaching position, since married women were not allowed to teach, although the same rule did not apply to married men. Terrell loved teaching, and she had a need to do more than just stay at home and take care of husband and children. Her husband sympathized with her feelings on this subject. Terrell's first three babies died after birth; her fourth child, Phyllis (named after the 18th-century African-American poet Phyllis Wheatley), survived; another daughter, Mary, was adopted.

Childbirth and childrearing delayed Terrell's activism, which at first took a distinctly conservative cast. Hence, when she became the first president of the National Association of Colored Women in 1896, which she helped found, she shied away from addressing such important issues as discrimination and racism. The association instead confined its goals to such noncontroversial causes as teaching better childrearing methods and raising money for the poor. Nor did Terrell make waves when she was the first African-American appointed on the Washington, D.C. Board of Education in 1901. She did, however, inaugurate a permanent, annual "Frederick Douglass Day" observance, the first of its kind in U.S. history, throughout Washington's public school system. How different was this woman from the one who wrote in her old age that

> . . . people who are discriminated against solely on account of race, color or creed are justified in resorting to any subterfuge, using any disguise, or playing any trick, providing they do not actually break the law, if it will enable them to secure the advantages and obtain the rights to which they are ENTITLED (Terrell 1940: p. 115)

Terrell's radicalism emerged gradually. With the founding of the militant National Association for the Advancement of Colored People (NAACP) in 1909, the tide was turning against Booker T. Washington's attitude of tolerance toward racism. Terrell became a charter member of the NAACP, and in 1919 she served as vice president of its Washington, D.C. branch. Even more influential in her awakening as a civil rights activist were her personal encounters with racism.

From the frustrations of trying to purchase a home in a safe, largely white neighborhood, to being fired from jobs during World War I because of her skin color, to being unable to eat or even go to the bathroom when and where she wanted, Terrell saw that racism was pervasive in the nation's capital. Nor could she, as a highly educated person and the wife of a respected judge, escape racism even slightly. As a long-time resident of Washington, D.C., she witnessed "Jim Crow" laws gradually and insidiously segregate the nation's capital. In the 1890s, it was still possible for her to eat in the restaurant of her choice and shop where she pleased. But this changed after World War I.

As a colored woman, I might enter Washington any night, a stranger in a strange land, and walk miles without finding a place to lay my head. As a colored woman I may walk from the Capitol to the White House ravenously hungry and supplied with money to purchase a meal, without finding a single restaurant in which I would be permitted to take a morsel of food if it was patronized by white people (Terrell 1940: pp. 383–384).

Without television or radio many Northern whites were unaware of the wholesale disfranchisement of black citizens that was occurring in the South. Terrell's education and public experience equipped her to speak and write with extreme effectiveness. She was always in demand as a speaker, and her writings were widely disseminated; moreover, she never shied away from speaking her mind. Not surprisingly, "Nothing delighted my heart more than to receive invitations to deliver addresses in the South" (Terrell 1940: p. 175), where she focused on such unheard of, even dangerous, topics as lynching, black disfranchisement, and the convict-lease system, in which prisoners, for the most part black, were leased out by the state to do grueling manual labor. Needless to say, they were treated like slaves by the people they were working for.

Before World War II, Mary Terrell was invited to deliver major addresses to large audiences in Europe. In Berlin, in 1904, she spoke in fluent German before an audience of thousands of women during the annual International Congress of Women. She was the only American who did not have to rely on translators. In Switzerland in 1919, she addressed audiences in fluent French at the International Congress of Women for Permanent Peace. Her aim was always to enlighten Europeans about the predicament of African Americans. "So great was the interest aroused in the Race Problem of the U.S. that requests for articles on the subject came from newspapers and magazines in Germany, France, Austria, Norway, and other lands" (Terrell 1940: p. 205). In Europe, she often compared Jews and blacks: "I said that just as the Jews are misrepresented and disliked in Germany, so Negroes were victims of falsehood and hatred in the U.S." (Terrell 1940: p. 207).

Mary Church Terrell in her sixties—author, worldwide lecturer, peace activist, civil rights leader, wife of the first federally appointed, African-American judge, Robert Terrell. (Library of Congress)

MARY CHURCH TERRELL

Writing was also an important avenue for getting across her point of view. In the 1920s, she took to writing popular short stories for children with a racial theme. This was unique in children's literature of that time. Her stories reflected true accounts of discrimination, based either on her own experiences or those of others. Because such stories were fictionalized, the white press felt comfortable publishing them. At times, with great difficulty, Terrell managed to have articles for adults published in prestigious, white publications such as the *Washington Post*, the *Washington Evening Star*, the *Chicago Tribune* and the *North American Review*. For the most part, major publications, even newspapers, rejected her writing as too inflammatory. They feared antagonizing Southern subscribers. British publications, on the other hand, frequently published her exposés of race conditions in the United States. Mary Terrell's lectures and publications at home and abroad served to educate the most influential people about the consequences of racism. She is remembered for setting the stage of the future civil rights struggle at home, and more important, for leading that struggle. Her political activism became more intense after World War II, in part because American attitudes, particularly in the North, toward racial discrimination were changing. Terrell also became more active because she was a widow, her children were grown, and decades of lecturing and writing had prepared her, in her eighties, to enter the arena of public protest.

In 1946, she sued the Washington, D.C. chapter of the American Association of University Women (AAUW) when it rejected her application for membership based on race. After a three-year court battle, Mary Terrell won the right to be admitted, and one more Jim Crow bastion crumbled. In that same year, she became an ardent supporter and advocate of the Equal Rights Amendment (ERA) for women. Gender equality for her was on a par with racial equality, and without equality of the sexes, she believed, racial equality would never be fully realized. She took to heart the plight of poor black women, who were discriminated against by virtue of their race, sex, and economic status. In 1949, Terrell spearheaded the campaign to collect 100,000 signatures to be presented to the United Nations Human Rights Committee on behalf of a black sharecropper, Rosa Ingram, and her two sons, unfairly accused of killing a white man in

Georgia. This campaign pressured the state of Georgia to retry the case, which resulted in the state overturning the murder convictions.

These victories spurred Terrell, at age 87, to initiate the fight against racial segregation in the nation's capital. No longer relying on moral arguments (although these were still important to her), she took to direct, nonviolent actions, such as organizing sit-ins, strikes, and boycotts of stores and restaurants that refused to serve African Americans. The federal government under President Harry Truman tacitly supported her cause, but remained aloof from the actual struggle to enforce equality.

In white gloves and a prim hat, Mary Terrell and three others, including a white Quaker, David H. Schull, entered Thompson's Restaurant in Washington. Only Schull was served; the other three filed complaints and took the case to court. While it took three years to win the legal battle to desegregate eating establishments in Washington, Terrell finally saw the end of segregated eating establishments in 1953.

In another battle, Mary Terrell—leaning on her walking cane and wearing a hearing aid—led picketers (during a snowstorm) in a protest against Kresge's dimestore in downtown Washington, D.C. Kresge's managers gave in to the formidable Mary Terrell and allowed black patrons in. Encouraged, she urged her army of volunteers to picket other stores. By 1954, segregated stores as well as theaters in Washington became a thing of the past.

On July 24, 1954, Mary Terrell died of old age in her summer home in Highland Beach, Maryland. Pampered and indulged as a child, she could well have become, in her words, like . . . "an unbelievably large number of the leading [black] citizens, manifesting no interest whatsoever in any effort to promote the welfare of their group" (Terrell 1940: p. 401). Perhaps pride in her attainments and her personal conviction, arrived at from the study of history, made the difference. Her fear that "the youth of the race may lose their faith in religion, unless the church takes a more active part in trying to bring about a better understanding between the racial groups" (Terrell 1940: p. 416) was also a strong motivation to battle against racism. Like other civil rights leaders, Terrell personified the truth that one individual can make a big difference. And Terrell became a hero of the civil rights movement in old age.

Chronology

SEPTEMBER 23, 1863	Mary Church is born in Memphis, Tennessee
1884	graduates from Oberlin College Ohio
1885–1886	teaches at Wilberforce University in Ohio
1887	is language teacher at M Street High School, Washington, D.C.
1887–1889	studies and travels in Europe
1890	marries Robert H. Terrell
1895	is first African American appointed to Board of Education of the District of Columbia
1896–1901	serves as president of National Association of Colored Women
1904	writes "What It Means to be Colored in the Capital of the United States"; key speaker at the International Congress of Women in Berlin, Germany
1909	serves as charter member of NAACP
1919	is key speaker at the International Congress of Women for Permanent Peace in Zurich, Switzerland; becomes vice president of Washington, D.C. branch of NAACP
1937	is key speaker at the World Fellowship of Faith in London, England
1940	publishes autobiography, *A Colored Woman in a White World*; organizes and leads protest movement that brings an end to segregation in Washington, D.C.
JULY 24, 1954	Mary Church Terrell dies of old age in Highland Beach, Maryland

Further Reading

By Mary Church Terrell

Terrell, Mary Church. *A Colored Woman in a White World.* Washington, D.C.: Ransdell, Inc. Publishers, 1940. A long but worthwhile autobiography. The book leaves off in 1940, with her most important civil rights work still ahead.

About Mary Church Terrell

Jones, Beverly Washington. *Quest for Equality: The Life and Writings of Mary Eliza Church Terrell, 1863–1954.* Brooklyn, N.Y.: Carlson Publishers, 1990. The author picks up where Mary Church Terrell's autobiography leaves off (but also discusses her life before 1940). Half of this book consists of some of Terrell's most important articles and essays.

McKissack, Pat. *Mary Church Terrell: Leader for Equality.* Hillside, N.J.: Enslow Publishers, 1991. Short account of Mary Church Terrell's life and times, beautifully illustrated, for young readers.

Sterling, Dorothy. *Black Foremothers: Three Lives.* Old Westbury, N.Y.: Feminist Press, 1979. A short, readable, illustrated account of Mary Church Terrell's life, along with the lives of Ellen Craft and Ida B. Wells.

William Monroe Trotter

CIVIL RIGHTS MILITANT
(1872–1934)

After a dramatic personal showdown in 1914 with President Woodrow Wilson over the issue of segregation, the outspoken William Monroe Trotter traveled to Chicago as a guest of Ida B. Wells' Negro Fellowship League. Wells wrote in her memoirs that other African Americans should stand behind Trotter in his fight for black civil rights rather than condemn him. She herself tried to make up for the lack of support by inviting Trotter to be her house guest in Chicago for 10 days. They had a lot in common. Both helped turn the tide against Booker T. Washington's popular theory that African Americans needed to accept discrimination and concentrate instead on "improving" themselves. These two fighters were the heirs of the black protest tradition of the abolitionist era.

Opposite: *Trotter, newspaper editor, founder of the National Equal Rights League (NERL), as he appeared in his prime.* (William Monroe Trotter Institute, University of Massachusetts)

45

☆ ☆ ☆

Into this backdrop, William Monroe Trotter was born on April 7, 1872. His family was quite prosperous and lived in the predominantly white Hyde Park section of Boston. Post–Civil War Boston was a paradise for African Americans compared to any Southern city and even to most Northern cities. Blacks could legally marry whites, for example, and segregation in schools and in transportation was prohibited. Trotter attended white schools, excelled in his classes, and in his senior year in high school was elected class president.

William Monroe Trotter inherited much from his father, who set demanding standards for his children. His father James Trotter was born of a slave mother and white plantation owner, and as a young man he enlisted in the black Massachusetts 55th Regiment and fought in the Civil War. Though just 21, James Trotter was one of only four black officers in the regiment. (Most of the officers and the commander were white.) Trotter helped lead the enlisted men in a protest over their unequal pay. The soldiers refused any salary until Congress passed legislation giving black soldiers the same pay as their white counterparts. Congress finally did so in June 1864.

After the war, Trotter's father returned to Massachusetts. He eventually quit his secure job as a postal clerk because he was bypassed for promotion in favor of a white man. He went into business for himself as a realtor. To qualify as a friend of the Trotter family, one had to share James Trotter's belief in racial equality and racial pride. An amateur musician, James Trotter found time to write and publish *Music and Some Highly Musical People*, a book on black musicians.

Trotter did not envision himself as a future civil rights leader. Instead, he was very religious and intended to become a minister, but his father would not have his only son preaching before a segregated congregation, white or black. And they both knew that no white church, not even in Boston, would ever engage a black minister.

Therefore, the young Trotter entered Harvard University, rather than a seminary, in the fall of 1891. The next few years turned out to be the happiest in his life, marred only by the premature death of his father. As his father's heir, Trotter inherited a considerable fortune but was careful not to squander it. In fact, he continued to be a model student, perhaps even too serious for his young age. His one fault seemed to be daredevil speeding on his bicycle, heedless of anyone who stood or walked in his path.

Trotter graduated from Harvard in 1895 at the top of his class, went on for a master's degree in liberal arts, but he was still undecided about what career to pursue. He turned down a teaching job in Washington, D.C., because he refused to teach in a segregated school. Ultimately he entered the real estate business like his father before him, made a comfortable living, and in 1899 married fair-skinned and blue-eyed Geraldine Louise Pindell (who nonetheless identified herself as black). Trotter's wife remained his close confidante and partner until her death 20 years later.

The couple lived in a comfortable house in a white section of Boston and were a socially active, ambitious pair intent on getting ahead in the world of whites. They were unusually religious, which may have been a factor in their gradual turn toward political activism. Trotter led the way in this regard. "'The conviction grew upon me that pursuit of business, money, civic or literary position were like building a house upon the sands'" (Fox 1970: p. 27).

The U.S. Supreme Court had overturned the Civil Rights Act of 1875, leading to the rapid spread of segregation in the South. By 1896, in the landmark *Plessy v. Ferguson* case, the Supreme Court even ruled that segregation was legal. Moreover, most of the justices on the Court were Northerners. Clearly, racial bias was not something confined to the South. African Americans still lacked a national organization to work on behalf of their rights. Booker T. Washington, an influential black spokesperson headed the Tuskegee Institute in Alabama, but he was far from being a civil rights activist.

Nonetheless, Washington's influence was immense. As a former slave and self-made man, he was a powerful role model. In 1881, with the help of wealthy whites, he founded Tuskegee Institute, which promoted the industrial education of blacks. Washington opposed most higher education for African Americans, which he believed made them unfit for practical work. In his view, blacks should "improve" themselves first and make themselves "worthy" before seeking equality with whites, which included the right to vote. In his famous "Atlanta Compromise" speech in 1895, Washington even gave his blessing to segregation.

Meanwhile, Southern white mobs in the 1880s and 1890s were lynching more than 100 blacks a year, without fear of arrest. Always afraid and reluctant to criticize whites, Washington blamed blacks for the lynchings. Such subservience angered and offended middle-class blacks in Boston, who constituted only 2 percent of the city's black population overall. And it also offended some whites, not all of whom shared the racist attitudes of the South. By now Trotter had begun helping with voter-registration drives in Boston. He joined the Massachusetts Racial Protective Association, and in March 1901, he helped found the Boston Literary and Historical Association. The black men who joined this group objected to the views held by Booker T. Washington. In October, Trotter gave his first public speech, which amounted to a full-fledged assault on Washington's views on race. He was unhappy, however, with merely talking about racial discrimination to an elite group of comfortable blacks. Trotter began longing for some action.

In 1901, Trotter decided to invest his money in a newspaper. Aptly named *The Guardian*, Trotter's weekly provided a forum for protest. Long before the phrase "black is beautiful" came into vogue, racial pride was the order of the day for *Guardian* readers. Trotter refused to carry a single ad that touted hair straighteners, skin lighteners, liquor, or tobacco. An opponent of Booker T. Washington called the paper "'the foremost race journal in advocating equal and identical civil and political rights for Negroes'" (Fox 1970: p. 31).

The Tuskegee supporters took note of *The Guardian's* appearance. Without an open declaration of war, the two contenders for the hearts and minds of African Americans began a struggle that resembled the biblical story of young David against the awesome Goliath. As the years went by, Trotter and his wife were forced to sell their home and sacrifice their savings to finance their paper (and Geraldine Trotter worked long hours as an unpaid "jack of all trades" in *The Guardian's* office). Without children of their own, they focused all their energies on dismantling the Tuskegee "machine," a highly influential group. Along the way, they made many enemies among blacks, especially the editors of black newspapers who felt they were going too far in their opposition to Booker T. Washington.

To say that Trotter attracted attention is an understatement. Even in liberal Boston, many whites didn't know what to make of him. When a group holding Tuskegee views, the National Negro Business League, decided to meet in Boston and invite Washington to address the group, *The Guardian's* supporters infiltrated the convention on the night of July 30, 1903. One of them threw cayenne pepper at the speaker's platform, causing violent sneezing. A battle ensued. Police arrived, arresting Trotter, his devoted sister Maude, and a few other radicals. A white journalist wrote a highly negative account of the "riot" and the "madman" Trotter that was picked up by newspapers across the country. Nonetheless, it made many whites aware, perhaps for the first time, that not all blacks favored Booker T. Washington. A few thoughtful white, and even staunch, supporters of Booker T. Washington, such as Oswald Garrison Villard, took note of the differences. The event also had a consciousness-raising effect on some blacks. W. E. B. DuBois, a well-known African American of his day, claimed that this event "Trotterized" him, leading to his final break with the "Bookerite" camp.

The radicals began to emerge as a force that the Bookerites had to reckon with. To compete as equals in wealth and influence, however, they needed the support of whites, whom Trotter refused to depend on. He allowed a few white people to join his National Negro Suffrage League but gave them no say. Without an effective national organization uniting most blacks, the racial situation continued to deteriorate. By 1908, the liberal white journalist Ray Stannard Baker noted that even in Boston, "'A few years ago, no hotel or restaurant in Boston refused Negro guests; now several hotels, restaurants, and especially confectionery stores [that sold sweets] will not serve Negroes'" (Fox 1970: pp. 34–35). The Tuskegee machine, its powerful group of supporters, refused to criticize even these injustices.

Taking note of the worsening racial climate, a number of rich, Northern whites took the initiative in laying the foundation for an organization that would help blacks defend themselves and their civil rights. This organization in 1910 named itself the National Association for the Advancement of Colored People. But the predecessor of the

NAACP was the Niagara Movement, a joint effort on the part of Trotter and DuBois. The black Niagara Movement was also a militant civil rights organization, but it ultimately failed because it lacked broad support and financing. By contrast, the NAACP was almost entirely white. The radical DuBois, who became the editor of NAACP's mouthpiece, *The Crisis*, was the sole exception. These white men and women at the helm of the NAACP—such as millionaire William English Walling, Mary White Ovington, Oswald Garrison Villard, and Rev. William Hayes Ward—were mainly Socialists, Christian evangelicals, and the descendants of abolitionists. They were far more radical than the white supporters of Booker T. Washington. The founder of Tuskegee would have been staunchly opposed to the NAACP's declaration, which described in uncompromising language the plight of "colored Americans," who were

> often plundered of their just share of the public funds, robbed of nearly all part in the government, segregated by common carriers, some murdered with impunity, and all treated with open contempt by officials (Fox 1970: p. 128–129).

Trotter had spent nearly a decade paving the way for such an organization as the NAACP, but when it finally arose, he distanced himself from it, letting his membership lapse and becoming its constant critic. He did not like the fact that the organization was led by whites; moreover, he, himself, wanted to lead such an organization. He continued to head his own civil rights group, which in 1914 adopted the name *National Equal Rights League*, or NERL. There was no real difference between the goals, message, and activism of NERL and the NAACP, but NERL never could compete with the NAACP for membership or money. But Trotter himself led the all-black NERL, and he would not take a back seat to anyone, not even to his friend DuBois. Nonetheless, Trotter continued to do what he was best at: taking fearless, courageous stands that many admired but few could imitate, even in the NAACP.

As head of NERL, Trotter met with presidential candidate Woodrow Wilson during the election campaign of 1912. Not a single African American served in Congress, but Trotter still was a firm believer in the power of the 750,000 African Americans, mainly in the North, who could exercise the right to vote. Trotter came away from his meeting with Wilson assured that he would keep his campaign promises to treat the Negro fairly. The NAACP also endorsed Wilson, but hesitantly: although Wilson had spent most of his adult life in the North, it was disturbing to the NAACP that he'd been born and raised in the deep South. When he won the election in November 1912, he swiftly appointed four white Southerners to his cabinet, which was taken as an ominous sign.

A year later, President Wilson approved Postmaster Albert Burleson's request to segregate his huge department, as a way of reducing "racial friction." For the first time in U.S. history, the federal government gave its official approval to segregation in the civil service, and soon Treasury Secretary William McAdoo, another Southerner, introduced segregation into the Treasury Department. When a dismayed Trotter led a delegation of concerned black citizens to the White House to bring Wilson's attention to this frightening turn of events, Wilson received him cordially. He listened carefully to the statement presented by Trotter and Ida B. Wells, which protested discrimination in the federal government. Wilson accepted their antisegregation petition signed by 20,000 blacks and whites from 38 states. Nonetheless, Wilson remained unconvinced that segregation was discriminatory. His view partially stemmed from the many approving letters he had received from African Americans— Tuskegee officials and other Bookerites. The prominent Bookerite Rev. Alexander Walters visited Wilson and assured him he was on the right track.

Twelve months later, in late fall of 1914, Trotter was back at the White House. Wilson had done nothing to halt segregation in the government, as Trotter had hoped. Once again, he led a small delegation into the president's office. For the next 45 minutes, Trotter tried his utmost to convince Wilson that segregation was degrading for blacks, but Wilson kept insisting that it only appeared to be degrading, that it benefited all blacks, and that a majority actually supported it. The president abruptly ended what was turning into an altercation. He was offended by Trotter's tone. No sooner was Trotter ushered out of the Oval Office than, to the press secretary's amazement, Trotter held an impromptu press conference with waiting reporters who were eager for a scoop.

Such audacity turned Trotter into a celebrity overnight. The amazed NAACP and the much smaller NERL congratulated Trotter. The Bookerites, on the other hand, offered the White House profuse apologies for Trotter's "rude" behavior. Nothing seemed to highlight the differences between the Bookerites and the NAACP's supporters more than Trotter's audacious confrontation with Wilson; it became a milestone in the struggle for civil rights.

More and more, Trotter, rather than his newspaper, came to personify black protest. In 1915, on the eve of the screening in Boston of the racist film *Birth of a Nation*, Trotter appeared at the theater with a dozen followers. Anticipating trouble, the movie house refused to admit any blacks, and police arrested Trotter. A few of his followers managed to elude detection and sat quietly in the audience: During a particularly offensive scene, they began hurling rotten eggs at the screen and even set off a few stink bombs before they, too, were caught and arrested. The next morning, Trotter, fresh out of jail, headed a protest delegation to the Boston State House, and later to the mayor's office. While his efforts to ban the film in Boston came to nothing (he succeeded in getting it banned from Boston in 1922, when it made its rounds again), the publicity that he generated helped the NAACP to keep the film out of other major cities. As usual, Trotter's daring tactics and the NAACP's growing clout set off alarm bells in the Bookerite camp.

Meanwhile, World War I was coming to an end, and after the cease-fire in 1918, President Wilson led a delegation of idealistic men to the Paris Peace Conference, where they intended to play a major role in the postwar settlement. Of great interest to Trotter and other African Americans was Wilson's plan to establish a League of Nations, the forerunner of today's United Nations. If the conference delegates accepted Wilson's plan, the League not only would keep future peace throughout the world, but also would recognize the rights of small nations and minorities, who would enjoy equal membership in the League. Since African Americans were a minority, Trotter hit on the daring notion of bringing the world's attention to the plight of American blacks. He called a conference of NERL in December 1918, which selected six delegates, including himself, to present a list of grievances to the Paris Peace Conference and to demand racial equality.

The U.S. State Department received word that Trotter's group was up to something and thus denied them passports to travel. All but Trotter gave up and stayed home; he was determined to make his way to Paris. Trotter haunted the wharves of New York City until he finally got hired as an assistant cook on an English freighter bound for France. What scared Trotter, though, was that he knew nothing about cooking. In desperation, he called on an elderly friend to help. With good humor she took him through a crash course in cooking. Thus outfitted, Trotter cooked his way to France. Landing at the port of Le Havre, he sneaked away from the ship, hopped a train to Paris, and made his way to the doorstep of a surprised African-American couple who didn't even know him, but who took him in anyway.

The next day, "'with the help of God'" (Fox 1970: p. 231), Trotter got to the Paris Peace Conference that by then was winding down. Trotter petitioned to meet with President Wilson, but not surprisingly, he was turned down. Next, Trotter headed for the major French newspaper offices and handed them press releases, announcing his arrival and purpose. Intrigued by this black American rebel whom they'd never heard of, articles began appearing in the French press, which took note of Trotter's desire to ensure that the League of Nations accept the principle of racial equality. In fact, a Japanese delegation had already tried and failed to get the Peace Conference to put a racial-equality clause into the League of Nations charter.

What Trotter accomplished in his three-month stay in Paris was, once again, to bring awareness of racial injustice to a broader public. The NAACP hailed Trotter as a hero and benefited from the publicity his extraordinary courage drew to their cause. Still, Trotter refused to have anything to do with the NAACP.

Nothing that Trotter did afterward ever equaled his Paris adventure. He spent the next 15 years living in poverty in Boston, but still publishing *The Guardian* every week. The paper went virtually unread and unnoticed, since it was unable to compete with the NAACP's flashier, better endowed publications. NERL was dying out as an organization, with many members "deserting" to the

An obituary photo of Geraldine ("Deenie") Trotter, which appeared in a December 1918 issue of the NAACP's The Crisis. *She died in the worldwide influenza epidemic following World War I.* (Moorland-Spingarn Research Center, Howard University)

NAACP. Trotter's devoted wife Geraldine died suddenly in 1918, a victim of the great influenza epidemic. It was a blow from which neither he nor his newspaper ever recovered. He became more and more of a loner, whose voice was muffled by younger, energetic men and women of the rival NAACP.

On his birthday, April 7, 1934, Trotter's body was discovered lying on the pavement near his apartment building. He was 62. Some thought that the sickly and increasingly weakened Trotter had fallen accidentally from the rooftop balcony; others suspected it was a suicide. The truth will never be known.

Although the two had long ceased to be friends, W. E. B. DuBois, who had stuck with the NAACP despite his frequent disagreements with its white leadership, wrote a long and moving obituary of Trotter in *The Crisis*. After sketching his life and career, DuBois summed up Trotter's racial philosophy.

> The Trotter philosophy was carried out remorselessly in his paper [referring to the *Guardian*]. He stood unflinchingly for fighting separation and discrimination in church and school, and in professional and business life. He would not allow a colored Y.M.C.A. in Boston, and he hated to recognize colored churches, or colored colleges . . . he lived up to his belief to the best of his ability (*The Crisis*, May, 1934, p. 134).

DuBois faulted Trotter only for "freelancing"—that is, ignoring the NAACP, the only effective nationwide civil-rights organization for African Americans, because of his suspicion of its white participants and members. Nonetheless, "Monroe Trotter," wrote DuBois, "was a man of heroic proportions, and probably one of the most selfless of Negro leaders during all our American history."

Trotter was remembered best for his selflessness, dedication, and heroism. Moreover, his religious faith guided him and gave him strength in his bitter battles against injustice. During the course of his life and long afterward, he was an inspiration to countless men and women who continued his struggle.

Chronology

APRIL 7, 1872	William Trotter born on the outskirts of Chillicothe, Ohio
1895	graduates from Harvard University
1896	earns M.A. degree from Harvard
1899	marries Geraldine Louise Pindell

1901	one of the founders of Boston Literary & Historical Association; begins publishing radical black weekly, *The Guardian*
1903	challenges Booker T. Washington at convention of Negro Business League
1909	becomes one of 40 original members of NAACP
1914	showdown with President Woodrow Wilson over segregation; his civil rights group takes the name National Equal Rights League (NERL)
1915	leads struggle in Boston against the showing of antiblack film *Birth of a Nation*
1919	undertakes illegal trip to Paris to bring the plight of African Americans to the attention of Peace Conference
1922	succeeds in getting *Birth of a Nation* banned in Boston
APRIL 7, 1934	William Trotter dies in Boston

Further Reading

About William Monroe Trotter
Adams, Russel L. *Great Negroes, Past and Present*. Chicago: Afro-American Publishing Co., 1984. Enjoyable, illustrated chapters on African Americans.

Fox, Stephen R. *The Guardian of Boston: William Monroe Trotter*. Kingsport, Tenn.: Kingsport Press, 1970. An excellent, readable, but lengthy biography that still is the only book about Trotter.

Sally, Columbus, *The Black 100—A Ranking of the Most Influential African Americans, Past and Present*. New York: Carol Publishing Group, 1993. One hundred influential, not always famous, African-American role models, for older teens.

A. Philip Randolph

FATHER OF MASS PROTEST
(1889–1979)

On August 28, 1963, one of the most memorable days in the history of the civil rights movement, more than 200,000 excited demonstrators crowded in front of the Lincoln Memorial in Washington, D.C., to hear the Reverend Martin Luther King, Jr., deliver his famous "I Have a Dream" speech. The man who stood ready to introduce King to the audience was 74-year-old Asa Philip Randolph. Randolph was a veteran of many bitter civil rights battles. To the astonishment of his closest friends who'd never seen him cry, tears trickled down his cheeks as he made the introduction. "This is the most beautiful day of my life," he said (Anderson 1974: p. 331). Randolph was tremendously proud that day of how far the civil rights movement had come. And although he would take no credit for himself, he was one of the people who had paved the way for King.

Randolph in the late 1950s, in this spontaneous newspaper photograph, taken just as he was removing his reading glasses. He was still president of the Brotherhood of Sleeping Car Porters and an NAACP activist. (National Archives)

Asa Philip Randolph (or A. Philip Randolph, as he signed his name) was born into poverty in Baldwin, Florida, on April 15, 1889. His mother Elizabeth was 17 years old when Randolph, her second child, was born. She had grown up with her siblings in a shack and married the new preacher in town, James Randolph, at 13. He was eight years her senior.

Neither parent had more than a few years of formal schooling, but James Randolph had educated himself and become an ordained minister in the African Methodist Episcopal (AME) Church, a denomination founded in the 1780s by freed slave and early abolitionist Richard Allen. The AME church's heritage of abolitionism and racial dignity always filled Rev. Randolph with pride, which he instilled in his sons. The town of Baldwin, Florida, was his first preaching assignment. Rev. Randolph's churches, even in Jacksonville, were tiny storefronts, and his congregants were poor but full of love for their preacher and his family.

Asa and his older brother James grew up in Jacksonville. Home life was strict, happy, and very religious. As one niece recalled, "'You couldn't eat a thing in that house without praying first'" (Anderson 1974: p. 37). Rev. Randolph had high expectations for his two boys, though he wasn't a strict disciplinarian like their mother. Fortunately there was a private, tuition-free high school for blacks in Jacksonville, the Cookman Institute. It was funded by Northern whites and was the only African-American high school in the city. Asa and his brother James entered in 1903. James excelled in math and Latin; Asa excelled in literature and sports and came to love theater and drama.

James Randolph's race consciousness affected his two sons: after public transportation in Jacksonville became segregated in the early 1900s, he insisted that they walk everywhere. When the public libraries became segregated, he forbade his children to study there. The brothers also had to become familiar with the writings of the abolitionists, which Asa Randolph cited later on as a major influence on his life. However, Randolph and his older brother rejected their father's religion and belief in a loving God, which seemed in contradiction to life's harsh realities. Nonetheless, years later as a union organizer, Randolph always started his meetings off with a prayer.

A. PHILIP RANDOLPH

Since there was no money for college and free public universities in the South would not accept African Americans, Randolph began working full time after graduating from high school in 1907. A Jacksonville insurance company hired him to collect premiums from its black customers, but he soon got tired of that. Thus, he began a restless period of moving from job to job. His reason for changing jobs so often was simply that they weren't worth keeping. "Is it only white men who can be bookkeepers and supervisors? Are we only good for sweeping floors and washing windows?" (Anderson 1974: p. 66). He began taking pride in the number of jobs he quit.

Civil rights were far from Randolph's mind in 1911, when he became fed up with Jacksonville. With high hopes of embarking on a stage career, he moved to New York City, where competition for acting jobs was fierce. He acted in amateur plays in black churches until one day he was offered a part in a major Broadway production. Pleased and proud, he wrote his parents in Florida about the offer. To his dismay, they were appalled at his becoming an actor, which to them was synonymous with a life of sin. Although Randolph was already in his mid-twenties, self-supporting, and in love with the theater, he made the painful decision to decline the manager's offer rather than alienate or lie to his parents.

He no longer had a good reason to stay in New York. But Randolph felt that African Americans could make a better life in the North, so he decided to remain. His acting experience in high school and amateur productions had taught him literature, especially Shakespeare, and he developed strong public speaking skills. His beautifully modulated voice would be an important tool that he would use later to win adherents to the civil rights cause.

Once Randolph decided to settle in New York, he joined a church club in Harlem for the purpose of making friends. One day at a club function, he learned that it was possible to go to college in New York for free—thanks to funding from the municipal government. Getting a college education, always a remote dream, now seemed within reach. He immediately enrolled as a night student at City College of New York (CCNY). Eventually, his brother James joined him, with the same purpose of getting a college degree.

Randolph never finished CCNY, but he became a Socialist through his college experience. In one of his courses, he studied the history of the European working class and the theories of socialism. Randolph was deeply impressed by the rationality of Socialist beliefs. Unlike any religion, socialism explained why poverty existed in the world, and quite unlike any religion, it insisted that, by means of organized action, poverty could be wiped off the face of the earth.

All Socialists agreed that poverty was caused by the exploitation of the poor by rich people who owned property. Economic competition among social classes in general was at the root of all problems, according to the Socialists. They said that the poor needed to stop competing with each other, join forces, and form trade unions (which the rich feared) to demand better working conditions. In this way, trade unionism would begin to eliminate poverty. Socialists in Europe and America were divided, however, on whether or not private owner-ship—from factories to one's own home—should be done away with altogether. Extreme Socialists, often called Communists, believed that all property should be owned in common by everyone.

Randolph believed that racism, along with many other problems, was a result of economic competition. In fact, Ida B. Wells, who was not a Socialist, had come close to this view when she theorized that the common factor in most lynchings of blacks was economic competition. She cited her personal experience with her close friend, storeowner Tom Moss, who was brutally lynched by white storeown-ers because he was competing with them.

Clearly, Randolph believed, God had no role in bringing about the Socialist utopia, when there would be neither rich nor poor. This was a much different view of religion than that which Randolph had been taught as a child. It was up to class-conscious men and women to make the dream real some day, by educating and organizing masses of working-class people. Randolph quit school and joined the Social-ist Party of America in order to do just that. Socialism became his new religion. Shortly after conversion, however, he married Lucille Green, a widow six years his senior, in 1914. After graduating from Howard University in Washington, D.C., Lucille became the very successful owner of a beauty parlor in Harlem. Randolph reasoned that the time had not yet arrived for a classless society in which no one owned property. Thus, he saw no contradiction in marrying a woman who owned her own business. Freed from personal financial worry, he threw himself body and soul into spreading the Socialist gospel.

For many years, he and his close friend Chandler Owen mounted soapboxes every day on the corner of Lenox Avenue and 135th Street in Harlem to proclaim the virtues of socialism and trade unionism. Because they were such good speakers, they always attracted an interested audience, including journalists of the *Jewish Daily Forward,* a newspaper that contributed money to Randolph's idealistic ventures. One day in 1916, Randolph introduced the firey Jamaican Marcus Garvey to his listeners. He watched with awe as the crowd took to Garvey and ruefully admitted that against "Against the emotional power of Garveyism, what I was preaching didn't stand a chance" (Anderson 1974: p. 137). In time, Randolph came to dislike Garvey's "back to Africa" message, along with the colorful uniforms and bands that followed Garvey everywhere he spoke. Moreover, Garvey didn't want to change the system and saw nothing wrong with wealth and property. Nonetheless, in a few years several million African Americans had flocked to Garvey.

Not for a moment did Randolph's faith in socialism falter. He opposed the U.S. government and all governments that he viewed contemptuously as being run by wealthy politicians who followed the orders of rich capitalists. After the United States entered World War I in 1917, Randolph took to the streets, protesting the "capitalist war," and began writing antiwar pamphlets. The government soon labeled him one of the "most dangerous Negroes" in America.

Like millions of other people, Randolph witnessed the Communist revolution in Russia in November 1917, which at the time promised the masses of Russian peasants, who had been little more than slaves for centuries, a better life. Idealistic Socialists in Europe and America expected the revolution to spread to their own countries. When Garvey's movement collapsed in 1923, Randolph felt vindicated. It seemed to prove that only profound economic and social changes in the current system would bring African Americans and poor white workers justice.

This was the message that Randolph preached in issue after issue of his radical black magazine *The Messenger*. Launched in 1917, it never attracted a large audience, but it drained all of Randolph's energy and financial resources. Nevertheless, the Justice Department in Washington took note of this "most able and most dangerous of all Negro publications" (Anderson 1974: p. 82). The government tried to shut it down, but failed.

Randolph's magazine caught the eye of several railroad porters, who sent a representative, Ashley Totten, to ask Randolph to organize a union for them. Totten approached Randolph in June 1925, but at first Randolph refused. First of all, he wasn't a porter; second, he didn't believe that a black union could succeed against staunch white opposition backed up by wealth and power. In fact, between 1917 and 1923, he and Chandler Owen had tried and failed at least a half dozen times to start up black trade unions in Harlem.

But Totten didn't give up. Randolph seemed like the perfect man to lead the porters: Because he wasn't one of them, the company couldn't threaten to fire him. Moreover, he was an eloquent speaker on behalf of black unions, a powerful presence, and even had a publication that could be used for the cause. As Totten summed it up, "No one in Harlem had a deeper understanding . . . or a greater concern for the problems of the black working man" (Anderson 1974: p. 108).

In time, Totten prevailed. Randolph's brother had been a porter for awhile. Randolph knew that the Pullman Company, which had instituted the first luxury sleeping cars, or "Pullmans," after the Civil War, hired only blacks as porters. The company counted on the docility of the newly freed slaves, who were hardly in a position to fight for their rights. Hence, their wages were shockingly low and their hours long; the porters were expected to pay for their own uniforms, meals, and shoe polish (shoe polishing was mandatory). They weren't even paid for arriving early on the job (a company requirement) to prepare for their long train journey. They were never addressed respectfully, which antagonized some of the better educated porters like Randolph's brother.

Randolph's task was a difficult one. The Pullman Company was extremely rich, influential, and inclined to fire any porter who made trouble. Moreover, the thousands of sleeping-car porters were scattered from coast to coast, and to reach them in an era when few people had telephones and few blacks had even radios would be a challenge. Even if every porter were contacted, the porters were poor, and membership dues for a union wouldn't be very popular or plentiful. Finally, even if Randolph could establish a successful union, the Pullman Company was not likely to sit down at the bargaining table with Randolph or treat the union with any respect.

Nonetheless, on August 25, 1925, Randolph officially established the Brotherhood of Sleeping Car Porters, with himself as president and the only officer in the union who didn't work for the Pullman Company. This was fortunate, since eventually all the other officers lost their jobs, and thousands of Pullman porters in the years ahead were fired for joining the Brotherhood. Although meetings were held in secret as often as possible, word reached the Pullman Company, which hired spies to be the company's eyes and ears. To make matters worse, most African-American churches and newspapers spoke against "Negro unionism." "Any Sunday you went to church the preachers touched on the Brotherhood. Their slogan was 'Don't rock the boat, don't bite the hand that feeds you,'" recalled one organizer (Anderson 1974: p. 184).

Ironically, white supporters of the Brotherhood were more numerous than blacks. White newspapers in the North wrote flattering accounts of Randolph and his able leadership. Meanwhile, Randolph used his connections with white Socialists and liberals on behalf of the Brotherhood, with the result that in 1925, a liberal white organization, the Garland Fund, donated $10,000 to the Brotherhood. In those days, that was a huge sum of money. It allowed Randolph to conduct a nationwide membership drive. Randolph consequently spent the better part of the next few years away from his tiny New York headquarters, traveling around the country, establishing local Brotherhoods, and raising the morale of porters through his inspiring speeches. Only a year after the Brotherhood's founding, the union had branches in 16 major U.S. cities from coast to coast. Randolph became tremendously popular among the porters and was in demand as a speaker, "the best orator I'd ever heard, bar none" remarked one overawed local organizer from California (Anderson 1974: p. 176).

Randolph's strategy of nationwide recruitment of porters, however, led to swift retaliation on the part of the Pullman Company, which in one day alone fired 30 porters in St. Louis for suspected union activity. The company even tried to get Randolph's picture taken in a compromising situation, by bribing women to entice him into their hotel rooms, or by disguising a spy as a policeman who would "arrest" him for some alleged offense, with a photographer standing conveniently nearby. Desperate to stop him, the company's attempt at a smear campaign against Randolph never succeeded. Pullman was much more effective at using spies to learn which employees were union members. Recalled one organizer: "If a porter had a fuss with his wife in the morning, the company knew about it in the afternoon" (Anderson 1974: p. 179).

Randolph tried repeatedly to get the company to recognize him as the legitimate spokesperson of the porters and to bring Pullman to the negotiating table. Even though Congress had passed the Railway Labor Act in 1926, which gave all railroad workers the right to form an independent trade union, Pullman ignored the Act and the Brotherhood. Randolph filed a complaint with the Railway Labor Board, but Pullman's lawyers argued that there was no proof that the majority of porters recognized the Brotherhood as their union. In fact, Pullman defiantly organized its own company union and coerced the porters into joining it with the threat that they would be fired if they didn't. Of course, this was illegal, but the Brotherhood did not have the funds to wage a long, drawn-out legal battle against the company.

Meanwhile, the Garland Fund's $10,000 was depleted. Randolph could easily have raised more funds from liberal white supporters, but he decided not to. Randolph had come to the conclusion that in the long run, it was in the best interests of the union not to rely on the help of whites: "This is one fight Negroes must win on their own" (Anderson 1974: p. 207).

The Brotherhood's dwindling finances, coupled with Pullman's harsh, retaliatory tactics against porters who openly supported the fledgling union, spelled disaster. Many porters began to feel that after three years of existence, the Brotherhood was ending in failure. Neither higher wages, shorter hours, nor better working conditions—Randolph's key promises at the Brotherhood's founding meeting in August 1925—had come about. The porters even stopped reading *The Messenger*, which folded in 1928.

To make matters worse, in 1929, the United States was plunged into the Great Depression, the worst economic crisis in its history, which would last nearly a decade. Bad economic times threatened to finish off what little was left of the Brotherhood. Porters were even more afraid than ever of losing their jobs. Consequently, membership declined from a high of 7,000 in 1925 to only 771 in 1932.

One by one, the branch offices closed down. Almost no membership dues came in from the Brotherhood, and Randolph's wife's hairdressing business had collapsed; thus, he went around in worn out clothing and shoes. A sympathetic colleague said of him: "He used to love his blue serge suit, which was the best thing he had, but he wore it so long that it began to shine like a looking glass" (Anderson 1974: p. 214). Yet, when the mayor of New York City, Fiorello La Guardia, offered him a full-time job in city government, Randolph politely refused. He explained to the perplexed mayor that he would never give up on the Brotherhood.

In short, Randolph remained an optimist in those dark days. He was still immensely popular with the porters, who did not blame him for failing. Meanwhile, Randolph tried to raise money and morale for the Brotherhood by organizing fundraising picnics, boat rides, and baseball games.

In the worst days of the depression, the tide was in fact beginning to turn for the beleaguered Brotherhood. In November 1932, Franklin D. Roosevelt was elected president. Henceforth the government would play an active role in pulling America out of the Great Depression by instituting FDR's "New Deal." The New Deal was a series of acts and programs designed to put people back to work. One of the first acts of the new administration was putting teeth into the 1926 Railway Labor Act. Section 7a of a new National Industrial Relations Act (1933) specifically granted the right of any employee to join a labor union of his or her choice. Under no circumstances could an employee "be required as a condition of employment to join any company union" (Anderson 1974: p. 217). In effect, Section 7a forced the Pullman Company to give the porters a choice—to join the company union or the Brotherhood. If they chose the latter, the company could no longer fire them. By mid-1933, less than a year after the Brotherhood's worst year, more than 8,000 porters suddenly joined the Brotherhood. Branch offices were reopened. In the summer of 1935, the Pullman Company reluctantly recognized the Brotherhood of Sleeping Car Porters as the legitimate union for the porters. The company reluctantly sat down with Randolph at the bargaining table. After long, drawn out, and sometimes stormy meetings, the Brotherhood, the first successful black labor union in U.S. history, triumphantly concluded an agreement with the Pullman Company on August 25, 1937 (ironically, the Brotherhood's birthday) that gave the porters more pay and shorter hours. Shortly afterward, the American Federation of Labor (AFL) accepted the Brotherhood as a fullfledged member. Almost overnight, Randolph became the most prominent black spokesperson in the country.

As far as the war-weary Randolph was concerned, he had just begun. "Without the porters, I couldn't have carried out the fight for fair employment, or the fight against discrimination in the armed forces" (Anderson 1974: p. 227). At this time, in India, Mohandas Gandhi was teaching a whole generation of civil rights leaders how to fight—and win—against overwhelming odds. Gandhi's tactics of mass civil disobedience, moral persuasion, and noncooperation had not yet been tried in the United States. Randolph was fascinated by Gandhi and his moral strategy, called ahimsa, which means "nonharming."

Randolph was increasingly disturbed that so few African Americans were benefiting from the economic recovery that was occurring under President Roosevelt's New Deal. Moreover, African Americans composed 16 percent of all military enlistments; yet all of them were sent to segregated army and navy units, where they worked at menial tasks. A year before the attack on Pearl Harbor in 1941, the Federal Security Agency published the alarming fact that "Over 500,000 Negroes who should be utilized in war production are now idle because of the discriminatory hiring practices of war industries" (Anderson 1974: p. 242). On January 15, 1941, Randolph wrote a press release calling on the defense industries of America and the federal government to halt their racist hiring practices. A meeting with President Roosevelt followed, but it turned out to be fruitless, since the president was not yet ready to challenge the status quo.

One day in early 1941, Randolph happened to mention to his close friend and fellow Brotherhood officer Milton Webster, "I think we ought to get 10,000 Negroes and march down Pennsylvania Avenue asking for jobs in defense plants and integration of the armed forces" (Pfeffer: 1990: p. 47). When he mentioned this idea to his other friends in the Brotherhood, the National Association for the Advancement of Colored People (NAACP), and the National Urban League, it caught like wildfire.

By March 1, 1941, more than $50,000 had materialized for the "March on Washington," as the project came to be known. Randolph was now calling for 100,000 African Americans to march on Washington, an unheard of and potentially dangerous gathering of blacks in the heavily segregated capital.

The thought of such a protest taking place in front of the White House upset President Roosevelt. He sent his wife Eleanor to reason with Randolph and even promised that he would write to all the defense plants to persuade them that it was their patriotic duty to hire African Americans. But Randolph sent the sympathetic Eleanor back to the White House empty handed. He demanded nothing less than an executive order; only then would he call off the march. The beleaguered President gave in gracefully. Appointing a committee of five, he instructed them to work out an executive order. On June 25, 1941, President Roosevelt signed Executive Order 8802, which required the defense industries and all federal government agencies to cease discrimination in hiring "because of race, creed, color, or national origin" (Anderson 1974: p. 259). The newly established Fair Employment Practices Committee would enforce the order.

The lesson of the March on Washington (which Randolph duly called off) was not lost on him and his followers. For the first time in American history, the federal government had been pressured into action because of the threat of mass protest. It was the same tactic that Gandhi had used in India, and it worked. Randolph publicly acknowledged his indebtedness to the great Indian leader and dropped his membership in the Socialist Party, which he had not been active in for years.

The armed forces remained segregated throughout World War II, but Randolph, who supported the war effort, was biding his time. In 1947, when President Harry Truman issued a call for a peacetime draft, Randolph was ready. He had established the League for

Randolph seated in the center, flanked by civil rights leaders (including Martin Luther King, Jr.) at the Lincoln Memorial, Washington, D.C., during the civil rights March on Washington in late August 1963. (National Archives)

Nonviolent Civil Disobedience Against Military Segregation, which threatened a mass rally of 100,000 in the streets of Washington, D.C. Members of this league also picketed the National Democratic Convention in Philadelphia, with Randolph carrying a sign reading "Prison is better than army Jim Crow service" (Anderson 1974: p. 280). The result was another Executive Order 9981 (signed July 26, 1948) that ended nearly a century of segregation in the armed forces. Once again, the threatened march was called off. Only a few years later, the Supreme Court would strike down segregation in public schools.

By that time, Asa Philip Randolph was in his sixties and had a serious heart condition. He began to devote more of his energies and spare time (he was still president of the Brotherhood) to the NAACP, making room for a younger generation of civil rights leaders.

At age 79, Randolph was mugged and robbed outside of his apartment in Harlem by three young black men. He bore no malice toward them, but the incident broke his heart as well as his health. He lived his remaining years alone (by then he was a widower), honored and loved by many. On May 16, 1979, at age 90, he died of heart failure in New York City.

As one friend remembered him, "He was a good man, a spiritual man" (Anderson 1974: p. 20) even though Randolph was never religious. But throughout his life, he cared deeply about the poor and the exploited. Randolph's greatness lay in his willingness to sacrifice himself for the good of others: "I consider the fight for the Negro masses the greatest service I can render to my people, and the fight alone is my complete compensation" (Anderson 1974: p. 151). He disdained personal wealth and comfort in order to do what had never been done before: organize a viable, black union in an era in which even white workers found it difficult to improve their working conditions and wages. When the Brotherhood of Sleeping Car Porters succeeded in 1935, Randolph did not rest on his laurels but continued his struggle for civil rights for African Americans, to the point of pressuring presidents of the United States to act on behalf of oppressed blacks. Randolph's tactics not only succeeded in ending segregation in the military and the defense industry; it also paved the way for the civil rights leaders who would succeed him.

Chronology

APRIL 15, 1889	Asa Philip Randolph is born in Baldwin, Florida
1907	graduates from Cookman Institute, Jacksonville, Florida
1911	leaves Florida permanently for New York City
1914	marries widow Lucille Green, beautician and graduate of Howard University

1917–1928	He and Chandler Owen edit and publish the *Messenger*, a radical Socialist weekly
AUGUST 25, 1925	Randolph establishes the Brotherhood of Sleeping Car Porters, a black trade union
AUGUST 25, 1937	Brotherhood scores first major victory against Pullman Company
JUNE 25, 1941	President Roosevelt issues Executive Order 8802, halting discrimination in hiring at defense plants and in federal government, thanks to Randolph's threat of mass march on Washington
JULY 26, 1948	President Truman issues Executive Order 9981 ending segregation in the armed forces, thanks to Randolph's threat of mass march on Washington
MAY 16, 1979	A. Philip Randolph dies of heart disease in New York City

Further Reading

Books About A. Philip Randolph

Anderson, Jervis. *A. Philip Randolph; A Biographical Portrait.* New York: Harcourt Brace Jovanovich, 1974. The most detailed and readable biography of Randolph.

Greenleaf, Barbara Kaye. *Forward March to Freedom: A Biography of A. Philip Randolph.* New York: Grosset & Dunlap, 1971. A 64-page, illustrated biography of Randolph for young readers.

Hanley, Sally. *A. Philip Randolph.* New York: Chelsea House, 1989. Concise, illustrated, and readable biography of Randolph for young adults.

Wilson, Beth P. *Giants for Justice: Bethune, Randolph and King.* New York: Harcourt Brace Jovanovich, 1978. Illustrated, interesting vignettes of three contemporaries in the civil rights movement.

Wright, Sarah E. *A. Philip Randolph: Integration in the Workplace.* Englewood Cliffs, N.J.: Silver Burdett Press, 1990. A concise, general history for young readers of Randolph's leadership of the first successful black trade union.

Thurgood Marshall

LITIGATOR FOR CIVIL RIGHTS AND SUPREME COURT JUSTICE (1908–1993)

On a cloudy, humid Sunday afternoon on January 24, 1993, 84-year-old Thurgood Marshall took his last breath in a stark hospital room surrounded by his loved ones. His great heart had given out at last. At his funeral in the majestic National Cathedral in Washington, D.C., few of the young people felt their elders' profound sense of loss or appreciated the enormous mark left by Thurgood Marshall.

"On the subject of the racial issue, you can't be a little bit wrong anymore than you can be a little bit pregnant or a little bit dead," the folksy Supreme Court Justice had once said (Hess 1990: p. 18). An uncompromising civil rights radical before Martin Luther King, Jr.,

Opposite: *Thurgood Marshall in 1965, after being nominated the first African-American solicitor general of the United States. Pictured with him is his second wife, Cecilia ("Cissy") Suyat, and their two sons, Thurgood Jr., and John.* (Library of Congress)

was even born, Marshall never once participated in a sit-in or civil rights demonstration. He was too busy litigating on behalf of the civil rights of all minorities.

The future Supreme Court Justice was born in Baltimore on a steamy hot day, July 2, 1908. He was named Thoroughgood, after his grandfather Marshall, a name he shortened to "Thurgood" in second grade because it seemed too long to spell. His mother Wilma was an elementary school teacher. His father William quit his job as a Pullman porter to become a waiter at the prestigious Gibson Island Club on Maryland's eastern shore, a club for whites only. Thurgood had an older brother named Aubrey.

Family tradition kept alive the memory of Thurgood Marshall's great grandfather, whom white slave traders kidnapped from Africa sometime in the 1840s. Both of Marshall's grandfathers fought in the Union Army during the Civil War, and both opened up grocery stores in Baltimore afterward, joining the sparse ranks of the black middle class.

Thurgood Marshall's childhood was happy and secure, and he grew into a mischievous child. In elementary school he misbehaved so often that the principal sent him almost daily into "solitary confinement" in the school's basement. Each time he was punished, he had to memorize a section of the U.S. Constitution. "Before I left that school, I knew the entire Constitution by heart," he quipped (Davis 1992: p. 37). He was surprised to learn that the 15th Amendment granted African-American men the right to vote, when nobody he knew, including his father, voted. He was also surprised to learn that the 14th Amendment granted all Americans equal protection under the law, since he knew this was not really so.

Marshall had his first bitter taste of racial prejudice at age 14, after he started a part-time job as a delivery boy for a Baltimore hat company. One spring day, as he was precariously balancing a high stack of hatboxes, he felt someone yanking him off the trolley car just as he was getting on, exclaiming "'Nigger, don't you never push in front of no white lady again!'" (Hess 1990: p. 18). Marshall not only lost control of the hat boxes, which tumbled into the street; he lost his temper as well and punched the white man. An exchange of blows followed until the neighborhood police officer, who knew and liked Marshall, came on the scene. That was the first and last time that Marshall ever resorted to violence. Instead, his brain became a potent weapon against racial injustice.

Despite his schoolboy shenanigans, Thurgood did extremely well, even graduating from high school early at age 16. Afterward he headed for Lincoln University, a prestigious all-black school in Chester, Pennsylvania. The school was established by a white clergyman in 1854 to give blacks an education comparable to whites. The entire teaching staff was still white when Marshall entered as a freshman.

That first year, Marshall clowned around a lot, playing pinochle or poker all night when other students stayed up studying for exams. Finally, the university expelled him because of his fondness for "hazing," or subjecting incoming freshmen to various forms of humiliation and pranks. Expulsion finally "got the horsin' around out of my system," he recalled (Hess 1990: p. 24). A semester later, he returned to school.

Hints of his future distinction as a lawyer were apparent in his brilliant debating career in college. He wrote home once, "If I were taking debate for credit I would be the biggest honor student they ever had around here" (Davis 1992: p. 46). Marshall soon abandoned all plans to become a dentist—a secure career his mother wanted for him—and turned his thoughts to becoming a lawyer. An incident occurred that convinced Marshall that redressing the wrongs of his people in a court of law would be his life's goal.

One Friday night, he and several of his pals headed for the cinema in nearby Oxford, Pennsylvania. Historically, Oxford citizens were always a bit uneasy about the black university in Chester, and officially, the Oxford theater was segregated. But Marshall's gang managed to escape detection and seat themselves on the main floor instead of in the balcony. Five minutes later, twenty more Lincoln students entered the theater and sat around Marshall and his friends. When an usher spotted them, he ordered them to move to the balcony, even though the movie had already started and nobody had complained. The students ignored him, but he wouldn't let up. Finally, Marshall turned to the usher and told him to let them enjoy the movie that they had paid for, like everyone else. Greatly outnumbered, the usher left them alone. From then on, Lincoln students sat wherever they wanted to in the theater. That tiny victory gave Marshall a taste for much bigger challenges.

By the time that he graduated with honors from Lincoln University in June 1930, he was already a married man. He had met beautiful Vivian Burey ("Buster") at a church social. It was love at first sight. They were both 21 and were soon married. Their happy but childless marriage lasted until Vivian's death from lung cancer in February 1955.

Though only in his early twenties when he graduated, Marshall was sure of himself and of what his future career would be. He had grown into a handsome man—standing 6 feet 2 inches, weighing a little over 200 pounds, and having fine silky hair.

Because he wished to practice law in Baltimore, it was logical for him to apply to the University of Maryland Law School. But the school promptly turned him down on the basis of race.

In the meantime, his only affordable choice remained black Howard University in Washington, D.C., whose law school lacked certification from the American Bar Association. When Harvard-educated Charles Hamilton Houston, Thurgood's future mentor, took the helm at Howard's school of law in 1928, he pushed through reforms that turned the institution into a first-rate, fully accredited law school.

In or out of the classroom, Professor Houston impressed on Marshall and his fellow students that "You are in competition with well trained white lawyers, so you better be at least as good as they are, and if you expect to win, you better be better" (Davis 1992: p. 55).

For the sake of free room and board, Marshall and his wife Buster lived with his parents in Baltimore while he commuted every day to Washington, D.C., 45 miles away, to attend law school. At night, he worked part-time jobs. Marshall graduated first in his class and had won Houston as a lifelong friend and partner. When Harvard University offered him a full fellowship for advanced legal study, Marshall turned it down in favor of "justice on a shoestring"—that is, serving African Americans, most of whom would be too poor to pay him.

The year Marshall graduated from Howard was 1933, the height of the depression. He operated his law practice out of his parents' home because his clients usually couldn't pay, and, thus, he couldn't afford an office. But he loved his work and was excited at each subtle sign of change for the future. A Jewish lawyer from the National Association for the Advancement of Colored People (NAACP) had written a report in 1931 that called for the Supreme Court to overturn its 1896 decision, *Plessy v. Ferguson.* This landmark court case had ruled that segregation was legal, so long as segregated facilities were "separate but equal." The *Plessy* case had paved the way for the Jim Crow laws in the South, which segregated blacks and whites in all public arenas—not the least being the public school system. In reality, wrote the author, "separate" was not and could never be equal, and therefore it violated the 14th Amendment that guaranteed blacks equality.

When Marshall's friend and mentor Charles Houston left Howard University in 1933 to head the NAACP's legal office, he began mapping out a strategy to combat segregation in the courts nationwide, particularly in education. Despite the depression, liberal white individuals as well as organizations were generously funding the NAACP. This support enabled the NAACP to carry out costly lawsuits in hundreds of cases of racial discrimination.

Houston recruited his gifted former student for NAACP work in Maryland. For the next two years, Marshall drove from Baltimore all over the state of Maryland—in many respects a typical Southern state—investigating cases of racial injustice, taking many of these cases to court, and even organizing boycotts against segregated Baltimore department stores. Marshall successfully sued for equal pay for black teachers, suggesting in court that as an alternative to raising salaries for black teachers, the salaries of white teachers could be lowered. After Marshall's victory against the University of Maryland's law school in 1935, which forced it to integrate, the *Baltimore Afro-American* hailed him as "the nation's biggest race man" (Davis 1992: p. 121).

In 1935, Marshall gave up his law practice in Baltimore to join Houston at NAACP headquarters in New York as his legal assistant. For the next ten years, Marshall, sometimes with Houston, traveled throughout the South to assess the state of black education and voting rights and to investigate lynchings and other brutalities against African Americans. Wherever he traveled in the South, Marshall sat at the back of the bus and ate in segregated restaurants. Marshall was biding his time, knowing that the situation in the South would change.

Charles Houston stepped down as head of the NAACP's legal office in 1938 because of his failing health, and Marshall stepped up to replace him. Two years later, the NAACP established the Legal Defense and Education Fund, a bigger, more ambitious effort to step up civil rights enforcement. Marshall headed the fund until 1961, serving as the NAACP's chief lawyer and winning several major cases before the Supreme Court. In 1944, in *Smith v. Allwright*, the Supreme Court declared that the "whites only" political primaries in Southern states were illegal. In Marshall's 1948 victory, *Shelly v. Kramer*, the Supreme Court knocked down "whites only" residential housing agreements prevalent in most U.S. cities. Arguing these cases before the highest court in the land gave Marshall invaluable experience for his biggest battle yet to come—on behalf of nationwide school desegregation. Until the NAACP could find the perfect test case to take all the way to the Supreme Court, the organization continued to patiently chip away at segregation.

With the end of World War II in 1945, human rights issues were in the news. The new United Nations charter even contained a human rights clause. In 1948, President Truman ordered desegregation of the armed forces, and a book by Swedish economist Gunnar Myrdal, *The American Dilemma: The Negro Problem and Modern Democracy*, which criticized segregation, had become a bestseller.

Unfortunately, in rural America, especially in the Deep South, many whites didn't care about human rights, and they continued to treat blacks badly, even the returning soldiers who had fought in the war. NAACP lawyer Thurgood Marshall discovered, on an investigative trip to South Korea in 1951, that even General Douglas MacArthur was maintaining a segregated army, in defiance of the law. "Every branch of the military was desegregated, but he [Mac-

Arthur] wouldn't budge," recalled Marshall (Davis 1992: p. 128). Clearly, overturning "separate but equal" would not be an easy task.

Everybody knew that educational resources for blacks and whites in the South were grossly disparate: for example, the state of Mississippi spent $117 per year to educate a white child and only $45 for a black child. Such statistics repeated themselves all over the South. However, getting a Supreme Court decision like *Plessy v. Ferguson* overturned after more than fifty years would take more than proving disparities in educational opportunities. Legislatures in Southern states could always decide (and several of them did) to improve black educational facilities to the point where, outwardly at least, they looked as good as those for whites. What Marshall and his staff had to prove was that the very concept of "separateness" bred a sense of inferiority among African Americans and opened the door to discrimination in many other avenues of life.

In the late 1940s, Marshall turned to Professor Kenneth Clark of Columbia University for help. An African-American sociologist, Clark had developed a convincing experiment that provided evidence of psychological damage stemming from segregation.

Mr. and Mrs. Briggs of Clarendon City wanted the best education for their five children. Harry Briggs, a World War II veteran, brought suit in court, demanding that the black public school in Clarendon County be brought up to the standard of white schools. Both he and his wife and other couples who joined in the suit were fired from their jobs. With Clark's help Marshall planned to appeal the case, if necessary, all the way to the Supreme Court.

Clark traveled to Clarendon City with Marshall and his assistant attorney and headed for the local black school. He brought one white doll and one dark brown doll to a classroom and asked individual boys and girls which doll was their favorite. He wrote afterward, "One little girl who had shown a clear preference for the white doll and who described the brown doll as 'ugly' and 'dirty,' broke into tears when she was asked which doll was most like her" (Hess 1990: p. 66). Only six of sixteen children preferred the brown doll. These data were used before the Supreme Court as evidence of the harmful effects of segregation on black children. White lawyers laughed it off, convinced that the justices would never take "the doll test" seriously.

They were wrong. Meanwhile, two other cases of discrimination in education came to the NAACP's attention: Reverend Oliver Brown in Topeka, Kansas, sued the Board of Education in 1950 for denying his daughter the right to attend a neighborhood white school, forcing her to take a long and dangerous walk over railroad tracks to the black school. This case, known as *Brown v. Board of Education of Topeka, Kansas*, would be combined with the Briggs case as well as a third case. The third case involved a young teenager, Barbara Rose Johns, who persuaded fellow students at her high school in Farmville, Virginia, to boycott classes as a protest against poor conditions in her school. All three cases came under the *Brown v. Board of Education* rubric. All three cases were lost in lower courts, which had upheld the right of states to legislate segregation. Thus, the NAACP appealed them to the Supreme Court.

Marshall, as head of the NAACP's Legal Defense Fund, never worked harder in his life to make the most compelling legal arguments that could overturn *Plessy vs. Ferguson.* He put together a conference of leading experts on the Constitution to get their views and opinions. Lawyers throughout the United States were solicited for their ideas. When the Supreme Court finally put *Brown v. Board of Education* on its calendar and was prepared to hear oral arguments in December 1952, Marshall was ready. The attention of millions of African Americans was fixed on Washington. The opposition was led by a brilliant, elderly white lawyer from South Carolina, courtly and persuasive John W. Davis.

Because of the complexities of *Brown v. Board of Education* and the explosive nature of the case, the Supreme Court ordered further oral arguments to be held nine months later, specifically focusing on the meaning of the 14th Amendment that granted blacks equal protection under the law. In the meantime, the aged Chief Justice and pro-segregationist Frederick M. Vinson died suddenly of a heart attack. Earl Warren, a liberal anti-segregationist, was appointed chief justice by President Eisenhower.

After the second round of oral arguments came to an end, Chief Justice Earl Warren, speaking on behalf of all nine justices on May 17, 1954, read aloud the Court's lengthy, much-delayed verdict to a packed chamber. Citing the fact that segregation and democracy were completely incompatible, he added: "To separate black children from others of similar age and qualifications solely because of their race generates a feeling of inferiority. . . . that may affect their hearts and minds in a way unlikely ever to be undone" (Davis 1992: p. 177).

A radiant Marshall (center) in May 1954, shaking hands with NAACP lawyers George E. C. Hayes and James M. Nabrit after the Supreme Court struck down Plessy v. Ferguson, *the 1896 decision that legalized segregation.* (Library of Congress)

THURGOOD MARSHALL

Warren proceeded to order the desegregation of public schools "with all deliberate speed." Henceforth, individual states would have little say over how the 14th Amendment would be enforced in their states.

To many, this verdict, which nullified *Plessy v. Ferguson* for good, was the most important Supreme Court decision in U.S. history. Justice Felix Frankfurter called it "a day that will live in glory" (Davis 1992: p. 179). A friend said of Thurgood Marshall that he was "so happy, he was numb" (Hess 1990: p. 74). Marshall's only regret was that his beloved former teacher and friend, Charles Hamilton Houston, had died a few years earlier. In the meantime, Marshall's wife had withheld from him that she was dying of cancer, fearing that this would distract him during the trial. She died the next year, February 11, 1955, on her 44th birthday.

Brown v. Board of Education heralded a time when racial discrimination would be illegal everywhere. Immediately, most Southern states declared their opposition to *Brown*. In the U.S. Congress, 19 Southern senators and 63 congressmen vowed to resist the decision. South Carolina filed suit in court (and lost), challenging the decision on the basis that it violated states' rights. The state legislature of Georgia declared that it would fight integration in all of its 159 counties. The NAACP's reaction to this stubborn resistance was further litigation to force compliance with the law. As head of the NAACP's Legal Defense Fund, Marshall initiated and won seven lawsuits involving resistance to *Brown*, all before 1960.

Right after the *Brown* decision, Marshall turned down a job from a prestigious New York law firm, which offered him an annual salary of $50,000, much more money than he was getting from the NAACP. Widower Marshall married Filipino American Cecilia ("Cissy") Suyat in 1955. The couple had two sons. Not until 1961 did he give up the NAACP to become a federal circuit court judge in New York.

Four years later, Marshall had proved himself so well as a federal judge that President Lyndon B. Johnson appointed him solicitor general, or the nation's chief lawyer, responsible for arguing cases before the Supreme Court on behalf of the United States.

When asked why he wanted Marshall appointed to this position, Johnson answered, "I want the world to know that when the United States speaks it does so through the voice of a Negro." (Davis 1992:

p. 248). And speak he did. In his year-and-a-half tenure as solicitor general, Marshall won numerous cases before the Supreme Court on behalf of the U.S. government that resulted in punishment of groups such as the Ku Klux Klan, who carried out racially motivated terrorism against African Americans and other minorities. When Supreme Court Justice Tom C. Clark announced his resignation in 1967, President Johnson considered Marshall to be the best candidate to replace him. After the Senate Judiciary Committee approved the appointment on August 30, 1967, he became the first African American to serve as a justice of the Supreme Court.

Supreme Court justices serve for life. "The only thing I have to do now, Johnny, is stay alive" (Davis 1992: p. 3), Marshall confided to a friend. He would be the staunchest supporter of civil rights in the Court's history. When he resigned for health reasons 24 years later, the Supreme Court lost its last remaining liberal and the strongest defender on the Court of the rights of minorities, women, and the poor. All the other liberal justices had died or resigned and had been replaced by conservatives, to Marshall's great disappointment.

Justice Marshall never lost his penchant for playing practical jokes. Once, when he was in the elevator reserved for the judges and some tourists mistakenly entered it instead of the one for visitors, Marshall coyly acted the role of bellhop, announcing each floor, and ushering out the tourists, who never guessed who he really was. He liked to greet Chief Justice Warren Burger, a formal, straight-laced man, with "What's shakin', Chiefy baby?" (Davis 1992: p. 8). But the whole Court knew that Marshall was dead serious when it came to his opposition to capital punishment (it was mainly minorities, blacks, or Hispanics who were executed), and his support of school busing to speed up desegregation.

To speed up integration, the Supreme Court in 1971 gave lower courts the right, whenever a public school was either all white or all black, to order busing of students to balance the races. Public opposition to busing, mainly from whites, was so severe that President Richard Nixon vowed to replace any retiring or deceased liberal justice with his own conservative choice. By 1974, despite Marshall's vehement dissent, or written opinion, the predominantly conservative Court reversed itself and put an end to court-ordered busing.

Marshall was the only Supreme Court Justice who had ever experienced what it was like to sit in the back of a bus because he was African American, and to fear Ku Klux Klan violence while he traveled alone through the South. Despite the real progress African Americans had made with the Civil Rights Act in 1964 and the Voting Rights Act of 1965, Marshall was not complacent. He knew how fragile the rights of minorities really were, and not just in the United States. Jews had been a persecuted minority in Germany, after all. When Marshall helped write Kenya's new constitution in 1960, he made sure that the rights of the small white minority there were guaranteed by law.

Increasing health problems and discontent at the conservative turn that the Supreme Court was taking—that is, rolling back achievements in civil rights—Thurgood Marshall announced his retirement on June 28, 1991 on the grounds that "I'm getting old and coming apart" (Davis 1992: p. 5). When reporters asked him about his legacy on the Supreme Court, he thought for a moment and answered, "I don't know what legacy I left . . . I guess you could say, 'He did what he could with what he had'" (Davis 1992: p. 382).

Marshall became a warrior for civil rights at a time when there were no civil rights demonstrations, no public outcry against lynchings and racial discrimination. Yet his legacy was profound. If it not for the landmark *Brown v. Board of Education*, segregation might still be legal. Moreover, Marshall's dedication to the cause of civil rights as well as his victories were an inspiration to black leaders who came after him.

Chronology

JULY 2, 1908	Thurgood Marshall born in Baltimore, Maryland
1929	marries Vivian ("Buster") Burey
1930	graduates from Lincoln University, Pennsylvania

1933	graduates first in his class at Howard University Law School, Washington, D.C.
1938	serves as chief attorney for NAACP, New York City
1940–1961	serves as first director and chief attorney for NAACP's new Legal Defense Fund
1954	wins landmark U.S. Supreme Court case, *Brown v. Board of Education of Topeka, Kansas*, which makes segregation in public schools illegal
1955	marries Cecilia ("Cissy") S. Suyat
1961–1965	serves as judge on U.S. Court of Appeals (Second Circuit)
1965–1967	is first African American to serve as U.S. solicitor general
1967–1991	is first African American to serve as justice on U.S. Supreme Court
JANUARY 24, 1993	Thurgood Marshall dies of heart attack at Bethesda Naval Medical Hospital in Bethesda, Maryland

Further Reading

By Thurgood Marshall
Marshall, Thurgood. "Oral History." *New England Law Review* (Spring 1993)
———. "Celebrating the Second Circuit Centennial." *St. John's Law Review* (Summer 1991)
———. "Commentary: Reflections on the Bicentennial of the United States Constitution." *Valparaiso University Law Review* (Fall 1991)
———. "The Supreme Court and Civil Rights: Has the Tide Turned?" *USA Today* (March 1, 1990)

Marshall, Thurgood; Mikva, Abner; Posner, Richard. "A Tribute to Justice William J. Brennan, Jr." *Harvard Law Review* (Nov. 1, 1990)

About Thurgood Marshall

Davis, Michael D., and Hunter R. Clark. *Thurgood Marshall: Warrior at the Bar, Rebel on the Bench.* New York: Carol Publishing Group, 1992. Written by two associates and admirers who bring Marshall to life in this detailed, factual account of his life up to his retirement from the Supreme Court.

Hess, Debra. *Thurgood Marshall: The Fight for Justice.* Englewood Cliffs, N.J.: Silver Burdett Press, 1990. Richly illustrated, interesting, and clearly written 115-page biography for the adolescent reader, with a brief introduction written by civil rights leader Rev. Andrew Young.

Prentzas, G. S. *Thurgood Marshall: Champion of Justice.* Broomall, Pa.: Chelsea House, 1993. A well-written biography of Marshall for young readers.

Rowan, Carl T. *Dream Makers, Dream Breakers: The World of Justice Thurgood Marshall.* Boston-Toronto-London: Little, Brown & Co., 1993. Detailed, highly informative, and readable account of the civil rights leader's life and times by Marshall's personal friend, journalist and political commentator Carl Rowan. Illustrated with photographs.

Rosa Parks

THE SPARK THAT LIT THE FIRE

(1913–)

Rosa Parks, an attractive, bespectacled seamstress of forty-two, worked as a tailor's assistant in downtown Montgomery, Alabama. At 5:00 the afternoon of December 1, 1955, she finished the last stitches on a pair of trousers, relieved to be going home. She grabbed her coat, fished for her hat, left the shop, and caught a downtown bus home. "The custom for getting on the bus for black persons in Montgomery in 1955 was to pay at the front door, get off the bus, and then re-enter through the back door to find a seat" (Parks and Reed 1994: p. 21). Parks sat down in the first row of seats behind the "whites only" section. Soon the bus filled up with whites. One white man was left standing with no seat. The bus driver glanced back and ordered all four black passengers in the front row of the "coloreds only" section to give up their seats. In Montgomery, if the white section filled up, blacks in the back were expected to give up their seats to whites. Not one passenger budged at first; eventually three got up, but not Rosa Parks. "The driver of the bus saw me still sitting there, and he asked was I going to stand up. I said, 'No.' He

said, 'Well, I'm going to have you arrested.' Then I said, 'You may do that' (Parks and Haskins 1992: p. 116). Little did Parks know on that eventful afternoon, when enough had just become enough, that her act of defiance was the beginning of a revolution that came to be known as the civil rights movement.

On February 4, 1913, Rosa Parks was born a year after her parents' marriage. Her parents didn't get along well, and when she was two and a half, Rosa's father headed North for a better life, leaving his wife Leona to fend for herself and their two children (Rosa and her baby brother Sylvester). Leona McCauley brought her children to live with her parents while she taught nearby.

Rosa Park's great grandfather had been a poor Irishman named James Percival, who had come to Pine Level, Alabama, before the Civil War to work as an indentured servant on the Wright plantation. As an indentured servant, he couldn't leave until his debt, or indenture, to the Wrights, who had paid for his passage, was paid off. Meanwhile he fell in love with a young black woman who was a slave on the Wright plantation. They married, and through hard work managed to save enough to buy 18 acres of land from the well-to-do Wright family after the Civil War. The Percivals were the only black family (they would have nine children) who owned their own property. One of their children was Rosa's grandmother Rose, whom she was named after.

Rosa's Grandfather Sylvester had bitter memories of the cruel white overseer on the plantation where he had lived, and thus he hated whites. "The one thing he wanted most of all was for none of his children or anyone related to him to ever have to cook or clean for whites." (Parks and Haskins 1992: p. 18).

Hence his daughter Leona, Rosa's mother, became a teacher in the black grammar schools of rural Alabama. At 24, Leona Edwards had

Opposite: *Rosa Parks at the height of the Montgomery, Alabama, bus boycott in 1956 that made her famous. Standing sideways behind her is the Rev. Martin Luther King, Jr.* (National Archives)

married a young construction worker, James McCauley, and moved to Tuskegee, Alabama.

Rosa and her younger brother were happy children. Their grandparents were a leisurely couple who liked to take them fishing and tell them stories. There were lots of farm animals to play with and plenty of trees to climb. "Pine Level was my whole world," recalled Rosa (Parks and Haskins 1992: p. 8). It was a tiny town with only three shops lining a dusty street and not a single railroad or bus line running through it. Pine Level was too small even to be segregated, but that didn't mean that blacks and whites socialized, or that there was no Ku Klux Klan. "At the time I didn't realize why there was so much Klan activity, but later I learned that it was because African-American soldiers were returning home from World War I and acting as if they deserved equal rights because they had served their country" (Parks and Haskins 1992: p. 30). Rosa's grandfather always slept with a rifle by his side.

By the time Rosa was old enough for first grade, she already knew a lot about racial discrimination. The school for white children in her neighborhood was brand new, with shiny windows and central heating in winter, and the children had their own school bus. Rosa's school, by contrast, was a one-room shack with only shutters for windows and a log stove for heating. Although Rosa's family was not extremely poor, there was no money to send the children to better grammar schools in Montgomery, 20 miles away, so Parks attended school in Pine Level. Perhaps because her mother was a teacher, Rosa could read by the time she was four, and she enjoyed school.

Grandfather Sylvester did not teach his grandchildren to hate whites. Instead, Rosa recalled, "I learned to put my trust in God and to seek Him as my strength" (Parks and Reed 1994: pp. 16–17). When Rosa finished sixth grade and could go no further in Pine Level, her mother enrolled her in the Montgomery Industrial School for Girls. This private school for African Americans had been run for generations by white women from New England. The religious values these teachers instilled in their students, however, seemed different from what most white churches preached in Montgomery. Rosa learned that "I was a person with dignity and self-respect, and I should not set my sights lower than anybody else because I was black" (Parks and Haskins 1992: p. 49).

As a result of their involvement with African Americans, Rosa's white teachers were shunned in Montgomery. Not even the white churches would tolerate their presence on Sundays. During the school year, these courageous women attended African-American churches, and in summertime, they returned to their homes in the North. At that time, the early 1920s, the school received its funding from the president of Sears, Roebuck & Co., a Jewish Northerner named Julius Rosenwald. He was deeply concerned with the plight of African Americans in the South, especially their lack of educational opportunities. He donated a considerable fortune to funding decent one-room schools for black children, known as Rosenwald Schools, throughout the Deep South.

After Rosa graduated from Montgomery Industrial School, she attended the private Lab School at the Alabama State Teachers College for Negroes in Montgomery. This was the only school available to blacks who wanted more education. Rosa's mother Leona paid for her high-school education out of her meager earnings, and she stayed there through the 11th grade.

Meanwhile, a young man had his eye on Parks, though the feeling wasn't mutual. "I just spoke politely to him and didn't give him another thought" (Parks and Haskins 1992: p. 55). His name was Raymond Parks, though he preferred to be called Parks. He worked as a barber in Montgomery, and what attracted him to Rosa was more than her physical beauty. Even at 18, she carried herself with dignity and pride. He knew from his own experience—he was in his twenties—that it was hard to find a girl or woman with race pride in heavily segregated Alabama. Though he had a meager education compared to his future wife, he was the first person she had met who was active in the National Association of Colored People (NAACP), which had only a weak presence in Alabama.

Rosa was 19 when she married Raymond Parks in Pine Level on December 18, 1932. Their close marriage lasted nearly 50 years, until her husband died of cancer in 1977. Right after their marriage, Rosa Parks continued working full time, but obtaining her high school degree meant a lot to her. So she returned to school at night and on weekends, and in 1933, she proudly received her high school diploma. In those days, very few African Americans in the Deep South graduated from high school.

Raymond Parks influenced his wife to become more active in civil rights. He was deeply involved in voter registration, a complicated, expensive process for African Americans. First, a literacy test was required. Rosa tried to register to vote for the first time in 1943. She was told that she had failed the literacy test—even though she had learned to read by the age of four and had a high school degree. Second, everyone had to pay a poll tax, but African Americans in Alabama had to pay the tax retroactively—each year from the time they had turned 21 (the legal voting age) to the year they registered to vote. When Parks finally became a registered voter at age 32, she owed 11 years' worth of poll taxes, but she paid. Finally, a white person had to vouch for an African American registering to vote. Parks was able to meet this requirement, but her husband never did succeed in getting registered.

By the end of World War II in 1945, Rosa was a leader in the Montgomery Voters League and the secretary in the local Chapter of the NAACP, whose president, E. D. Nixon, was working as a Pullman porter. Nixon had organized the Alabama branch of A. Phillip Randolph's Brotherhood of Sleeping Car Porters and also headed that local office. Parks loved her job at the NAACP: "I recorded and sent membership payments to the national office, answered telephones, wrote letters, sent out press releases, and kept a record of cases of violence against black people" (Parks and Haskins 1992: p. 84). In addition, she headed the NAACP Youth Council, which attempted to draw youngsters into the sphere of the NAACP's activities. "One of our projects was getting the young people to try to take out books from the main library instead of going to the little branch across town that was the colored library" (Parks and Haskins 1992: p. 94).

For all of these responsibilities, including her work for the Voters League, Parks received no pay. When Nixon asked her to volunteer as his part-time assistant in the Brotherhood of Sleeping Car Porters' local office, Parks gladly accepted. Her full-time job as a seamstress could never provide the personal fulfillment that her volunteer work did.

Through Nixon, Parks met Virginia Durr, a white woman whose father had been a minister in Montgomery. She was the wife of Clifford Durr, a prominent lawyer. Because of their interest in civil rights, they were an unpopular couple in white Montgomery. Durr encouraged her to apply to the Highlander School in Tennessee, run by Myles Horton, a white man deeply committed to social justice. "The school offered workshops to train future leaders so they could go back home and work for change using what they had learned at the school" (Parks and Haskins 1992: p. 103), recalled Rosa, who attended classes there every summer.

Nonetheless, on the day she was arrested for refusing to give up her seat to a white man, Parks didn't have any intention of making waves. She was tired and looking forward to dinner with her husband and mother at home. But her real fatigue was not physical. "All I felt was tired. Tired of being pushed around . . . Tired of the Jim Crow laws. Tired of being oppressed. I was just plain tired" (Parks and Reed 1994: p. 17).

As Rosa Parks sat in jail in Montgomery on the evening of her arrest, word of her plight spread quickly. A few hours later, her husband arrived, bringing with him Nixon and the Durrs, who got her out of jail. Virginia Durr gave her friend a bear hug, which shocked everyone; whites were not supposed to show affection to blacks in segregated Alabama. Meanwhile, Nixon was secretly thanking God that he had finally found the right person to challenge segregated busing in Montgomery. "'This avid church-goer looked like the symbol of Mother's Day'" (Wright 1991: p. 38), recalled a friend about Parks, whom everyone knew and loved.

At home with her husband and mother, Rosa wasn't at all sure she wanted to become a "test case" against segregated busing and have her life turned upside down. To be sure, she knew she would never take another city bus again. But did she want to become the focal point of a citywide boycott of the bus system?

By morning she had made up her mind to go along with Nixon. Her decision took great courage, as the weeks and months ahead would show. The boycott brought to prominence a young, new preacher in town, Martin Luther King, Jr., and resulted in a Supreme Court decision ruling segregated busing in Montgomery unconstitutional. That would be just the beginning. "I had no idea when I refused to give up my seat on that Montgomery bus that my small action would help put an end to the segregation laws in the South" (Parks and Haskins 1992: p. 2).

On the Sunday following Rosa Parks' arrest, all African-American churches in Montgomery urged their congregants to boycott the buses the next day, December 5, when Parks was to stand trial. Church volunteers distributed 35,000 leaflets to passers-by urging them to stay off the buses. As a result, African-American bus riders, constituting 66 percent of the bus company's customers, found alternative ways to get to work on Monday.

The Monday boycott was a dazzling success. Rosa Parks was tried and, after a brief trial, found guilty, a verdict that enabled her lawyers to appeal her case, if need be, all the way to the Supreme Court. That evening a tumultuous gathering filled the Holt Street Baptist Church inside and out, as the question of whether to continue the boycott was considered. In just a few days' time, Rev. Ralph Abernathy and other pastors in Montgomery had formed the Montgomery Improvement Association (MIA), to lead a prolonged bus boycott, should it come to that. The new pastor of the Dexter Avenue Baptist Church, Martin Luther King, Jr., agreed to serve as the MIA's president. That evening, he delivered the first of many memorable speeches, laying down the principles of love and nonviolence that would guide the forthcoming struggle. The crowd in the church resoundingly approved the boycott's continuation.

"The boycott lasted through that week, and then through the next. No one had any idea how long it would last" (Parks and Haskins 1992: pp. 141–142). Its resumption was met with intense hostility by the bus company, as well as by the mayor and city council of Montgomery. White churches remained silent throughout, perhaps to avoid the fate of one Lutheran pastor in town, Reverend Robert Graetz, whose public support of the boycott led white supremacists to bomb his home.

Meanwhile, the Parks' lives were turned upside down. Raymond Parks lost his job as a barber, and Rosa lost hers as a seamstress. Rosa's mother got in the habit of answering the phone, to spare her daughter and son-in-law from hearing the many death threats and hate calls.

Parks was thankful that her apartment was never bombed, as Nixon's and King's homes in Montgomery would be. Meanwhile, deep religious faith sustained her throughout the whole ordeal. "I felt the Lord would give me the strength to endure whatever I had to face. God did away with all my fear" (Parks and Reed 1994: p. 17).

Rides had to be found for the thousands of African Americans stranded without bus transportation. The churches were innovative

Rosa Parks being fingerprinted at the police station in Montgomery by a white police officer. This was a second, brief, arrest at the height of the bus boycott in 1956, and photographers were ready. (Library of Congress)

ROSA PARKS

in their approach to this problem—mobilizing taxi drivers who were willing to charge the 10-cent bus fare, and persuading blacks who owned cars to volunteer as drivers during rush hour. Some church congregations raised money for the purchase of church station wagons to help out the boycotters. In this way, some 30,000 former bus riders stayed off Montgomery's buses during the more than year-long boycott. Many wealthy white women sympathized with the boycott and willingly drove blacks working as domestics in their homes to and from work, even though the mayor asked them not to do so.

In February 1956, an appeals court threw out Rosa Parks' conviction on a technicality, making further appeals impossible. Clifford Durr suggested another way to contest the constitutionality of Montgomery's segregated busing law—by suing the bus company in federal court. The MIA wisely took his counsel. Because of his pro-boycott sympathies, Clifford Durr lost his white clientele, and his law practice went bankrupt.

Months later, the lawsuit was taken up by the Supreme Court in Washington, D.C. On November 13, 1956, the Court announced its verdict: that segregated busing in Montgomery, Alabama, was unconstitutional and illegal. The bus company would be forced to integrate or shut down. While the Court's decision took another five weeks to become official, it arrived just in time: white-owned insurance companies were refusing to renew auto insurance on vehicles, including church station wagons, that were helping out the boycotters. Montgomery's mayor triumphantly got a court order to prevent boycotters from gathering on their designated street corners, where various taxicabs, station wagons, and private cars picked them up and took them to work. The mayor seemed willing to do anything to stop integration.

The long suffering boycotters, including Rosa Parks and King, could hardly believe they were victorious. The 381-day boycott was finally over. Rosa Parks described the end of the long bus boycott very matter of factly:

> The boycott had lasted more than a year. Dr. King, the Reverend Abernathy, Mr. Nixon, and Glen Smiley, one of the few white people in Montgomery who had supported the boycott, made

a great show of riding the first integrated bus in Montgomery. Some of the books say I was with them, but I was not (Parks and Haskins 1992: p. 137).

Rosa Parks was home that day, nursing her sick mother.

But desegregation wasn't followed by wholehearted integration; nor would peace be restored between the races for a long time to come. Whites in Montgomery tried and failed to get a "whites only" private bus line established; the disgruntled mayor imposed a curfew on all city buses to prevent African Americans from riding home from work; angry whites occasionally shot at passing buses. The hate calls continued, forcing Parks, her husband, and mother in 1957 to leave Alabama for good and begin a new life in Detroit.

Parks returned to the South many times, however. Her courageous actions as a private citizen sparked a civil rights movement throughout the South that would finally lead to the enforcement of civil rights for all citizens. Parks never missed a civil rights march nor an occasion to speak in public. She was much sought after as a speaker. People all over the country were eager to hear from her own lips, not about the "incident" on the bus that would change American history, but what lay behind her quiet, unassuming heroism.

The Parkses led a good life in Detroit. Raymond Parks quickly found employment as a barber, while Rosa was hired in 1965 by Congressman John Conyers of Michigan, for whom she worked until her retirement in 1988. For a long time she had dreamed of establishing "some kind of organization to help young people" (Parks and Haskins 1992: pp. 181–182), to give them hope for the future. In 1987, the widowed Rosa Parks fulfilled her dream when she co-founded, along with her friend Elaine Steele, the Rosa and Raymond Parks Institute for Self-Development. With the help of grants and her own funds, the institute opened its doors to Detroit's youth, providing continuing-education, athletic, and counseling programs.

In late August of 1994, Rosa Parks made headlines again, when it was revealed that she had been mugged by a young African-American man who broke into her home in Detroit. The next day, newspapers from coast to coast reported the break-in and assault of the civil rights hero.

In her sunset years, Rosa Parks has spent time doing what she has always done best—good works. She also wrote two inspirational books about her life and struggles, which are full of wisdom and religious faith. She also has traveled the world over, from Sweden to Japan, to receive "more honorary degrees and plaques and awards than I can count" (Parks and Haskins 1992: p. 185). Rosa Parks will be remembered as the spark that lit a fire that became one of the largest civil rights movements in history.

Chronology

FEBRUARY 4, 1913	Rosa Parks is born in Tuskegee, Alabama
1932	marries Raymond Parks in Pine Level, Alabama
1933	receives high-school diploma
1943	for the first time, tries and fails to register to vote in Alabama
1945	succeeds in becoming registered voter; serves as secretary of Montgomery NAACP
1949	serves as adviser to NAACP Youth Council
1955	spends summer at Highlander School, Tennessee, and learns civil disobedience tactics
DECEMBER 1, 1955	refuses to give up seat to a white person on bus in Montgomery; arrested and jailed
DECEMBER 5, 1955– DECEMBER 20, 1956	Montgomery bus boycott occurs; Rosa Parks and husband lose their jobs; Supreme Court declares segregated busing in Montgomery unconstitutional
1957	Rosa and husband move to Detroit
1963–1965	Parks participates in major civil rights marches and is present at the March on Washington in August 1963

1965–1988	works for African-American congressman from Michigan, John Conyers
1987	cofounds Rosa and Raymond Parks Institute for Self-Development for disadvantaged youths in Detroit
1992	publishes first book, *Rosa Parks, My Story*
1994	publishes second book, *Quiet Strength*; receives honorary doctoral degree from Soka University, Japan; trip to Stockholm, Sweden, to receive Rosa Parks Peace Prize

Further Reading

By Rosa Parks

Parks, Rosa and Haskins, Jim. *Rosa Parks, My Story*. New York: Dial Books, 1992. Simply told but powerfully written account of her life, complete with photographs.

Parks, Rosa and Reed, Gregory J. *Quiet Strength, The Faith, the Hope, and the Heart of a Woman Who Changed a Nation*. Grand Rapids, Mich.: Zondervan Publishing House, 1994. Philosophical and witty reflections of Rosa Parks in her senior years.

Books About Rosa Parks

Benjamin, Anne. *Young Rosa Parks: A Civil Rights Heroine*. Mahwah, N.J.: Troll Associates, 1995. Fascinating story of Rosa Parks' life and the Montgomery bus boycott, written and illustrated for young people.

Hughes Wright, Roberta. *The Birth of the Montgomery Bus Boycott*. Southfield, Mich.: Charro Press, 1991. Gripping account of the 381-day bus boycott in Montgomery and the role that, not only Rosa Parks, but many others, played in it.

Hull, Mary. *Rosa Parks*. New York: Chelsea House, 1994. Sensitively written and inspiring biography of Rosa Parks for young people.

Fannie Lou Hamer

FROM SHARECROPPER TO ACTIVIST
(1917–1977)

One very hot Sunday morning in August 1962, Fannie Lou Hamer, cotton picker, part-time cleaning lady, and laundress, was sitting in church next to her husband. The pastor's sermon droned on and on. Children grew restless, while the open windows let in more heat and flies than air. Hamer's mind wandered to her many tasks that had to be done in the week ahead, to unpaid bills, to the joys and headaches of raising her two adopted children. Suddenly her ears caught the unfamiliar words, "mass meeting." It would take place in the church the next evening. "'Well, I didn't know what a 'mass meeting' was. I was just curious to go, so I did'" (Colman 1993: p. 13). Next evening Hamer showed up with a handful of other curiosity seekers. "'I heard it was our right as human beings to register to vote. I didn't know black people could vote. Nobody ever told me'" (Colman 1993: p. 13). The life of this 44-year-old field worker from Ruleville, Mississippi was suddenly turned upside down.

Opposite: *Fannie Lou Hamer in 1964.* (Library of Congress)

☆ ☆ ☆

Fannie Lou, 20th child of her parents, Jim and Ella Townsend, was born on October 6, 1917. Her birth took the family through a particularly grim winter in Montgomery County, Mississippi.

Hope was hard to come by in the Mississippi Delta, even if you were white but as poor as your black neighbors. Sharecropping was a way of life for most poor rural inhabitants of that rich, black-earth region of northwestern Mississippi. Because cotton brought big profits to plantation owners, there was no incentive to develop any other kind of industry. Moreover, mechanized cotton picking seemed unnecessary, when manual labor was so cheap. Wealth derived not only from cotton but from the fat government subsidies, or farm payments, that plantation owners received annually. For the most part, their lives were ones of ease and comfort.

Fannie Lou's parents, too, were sharecroppers. Sharecropping meant that in exchange for a rundown house without plumbing and electricity, sharecroppers had to buy their own fertilizer and cotton seed, plant the seed themselves, and "share" half of the harvest with the plantation owner. For each child born to a sharecropping family, the plantation owner would "reward" the parents with a bonus of $50, since children were assuring a cheap future workforce.

So many black sharecroppers left the cotton fields for jobs in the North during World War I (1914–1918) that Hamer's parents decided to take advantage of the shortage left by departing field hands. They headed further south, where wages were slightly higher, and ended up sharecropping on a plantation outside of tiny Ruleville, in Sunflower County, Mississippi. With so many mouths to feed, Hamer's parents could not provide the children with shoes. Her mother would wrap rags around her children's feet. At age six, Hamer started picking cotton. At age eight, she told her mother how much she wished she'd been born white instead of black. To her surprise, her poor mother sternly rebuked her: "'Don't feel like that. You respect yourself as a black child. And when you're grown . . . you respect yourself as a black woman, and other people will respect you'" (Colman 1993: p. 12). Hamer always remembered that early lesson and held her head high from then on.

Fannie Lou Hamer started picking cotton full time—with five months off for school—when she turned six. School ended when she finished sixth grade. An exceptionally bright child, she'd learned to read and do arithmetic. Writing, on the other hand, was an art she never mastered. Her English remained ungrammatical, so much so that, on one occasion, a highly educated civil-rights speaker was too embarrassed to be seen standing beside her on the same podium. Everyone she grew up with spoke like her, so Hamer never felt handicapped until she embarked on her civil rights career.

Typically, she married a sharecropper—friendly, easygoing Perry ("Pap") Hamer, when she was 27 and he was 32. They never had children. With both of them working full time, money still was hard to come by, because wages were so low. The couple adopted two children, one of whom had suffered bad burns in a fire. People came to Hamer with their problems because they always found a good listener. At one point, Hamer was promoted to timekeeper on the Marlowe plantation. Otherwise, life went on while the winds of change were blowing out of Montgomery, Alabama.

There were no buses, train stations, or trains in any of the little towns in the Delta. If you were a poor black or white, you stayed in the same place all your life.

Hardscrabble poverty and resignation were the keynotes of Hamer's life on that fateful day when, driven by curiosity, she attended a "mass meetin'" for the first time in her life. She'd heard of the "Freedom Riders," as civil rights activists from the North were called, even though they had never come to Ruleville or any of the other surrounding hamlets. For the first time, she heard of the Southern Christian Leadership Conference (SCLC) and of the Student Non-Violent Coordinating Committee (SNCC, pronounced "snick"), whose representatives organized that meeting. Suddenly, it was like a veil lifted from her eyes and she could see that her life could be different, merely by exercising her right to vote. If all blacks of voting age in Sunflower County (where no African Americans voted at all) became registered voters, things would change for the better.

Many other poor rural blacks—along with highly educated, urban blacks—had heard the same message. Very few decided to risk everything and become registered voters. Hamer asked herself, what did she really have? Not even security. Ever since a brutal lynching occured in the neighboring town of Doddsville in 1904, reported even in New York newspapers, no African Americans in the area ever spoke up for their rights. The Ku Klux Klan, and not the NAACP, was a household word. Now and then hooded Klansmen would ride by at night, with guns bristling from an open-air car. The Mississippi Delta was the world's most oppressive place to live if you were black.

Hamer clearly was different from many of her black rural neighbors. Without the slightest doubt, she believed what SNCC organizers told her about her rights. On August 31, she and 17 others boarded a big yellow bus to the county seat of Indianola. They would try to register to vote.

Nowadays, registering to vote is as easy as checking out a library book. In the Deep South in the days before the Voting Rights Act of 1965, registering to vote was so complicated that many whites were discouraged from registering as well, especially poor ones. A person couldn't just register to vote in his or her town or neighborhood. That would make it too easy for blacks to learn about voting. Hence, registering meant traveling some distance to the county courthouse during work hours (voter registration rarely took place on weekends), standing in long lines, taking a literacy test, paying a poll tax (which blacks and poor whites rarely could afford), and for blacks, there were further humiliations. Consequently, on the day she finally had the opportunity to register, Hamer passed the literacy test, paid the poll tax, answered the lengthy questionnaire, but when she was asked to interpret a part of the state constitution on "'facto laws, and I knowed as much about a facto law as a horse knows about Christmas Day,'" she knew she wouldn't be able to register (Mills 1993: p. 37).

The day after she returned on the yellow bus from Indianola, she encountered her boss, Marlowe. Word of her audacity had spread like a flash of lightning. He ordered her off his property by sundown if she tried to register again. That night, she fled to a friend's house. Ten days later, 16 shots were fired in the dark, straight through the house. Miraculously, no one was injured. Perry Hamer, who had been secretly visiting his wife, soon was fired from his job and evicted, along with their two children. When asked once why she never left

Mississippi, Hamer answered simply, "'You don't run away from the problems, you just face them'" (Colman 1993: p. 18).

Fannie Lou Hamer proudly became a field worker for SNCC. The meager salary they paid her, 10 dollars per week, barely kept her family alive, since her husband could not get hired after his eviction. But working for a cause she believed put a sparkle in her eye and a joy in her heart that amply compensated for the low pay. She taught citizenship classes, visited people to encourage them to register, and gave talks in the area—especially about what it felt like to lose your job just because you wanted to be a good citizen. After hearing her talk one day, an African-American lawyer was moved to say, "'You never needed to hear anybody else speak again'" (Mills 1993: p. 85).

The day she finally succeeded in registering to vote, Klansmen rode by her rented shack. Night after night they came, slowly and delib-

Black and white SNCC workers conducting a house-to-house voter registration drive in Hamer's hometown of Ruleville, Mississippi. SNCC recruited her in 1962.
(National Archives)

FANNIE LOU HAMER

erately driving around the house, a silent, gruesome procession. Yet they refrained from firing any shots, perhaps because white SNCC workers often lived and slept with her family, a shocking spectacle to whites and blacks in segregated Sunflower County.

In June 1963, SNCC sent Fannie Lou Hamer to Charleston, South Carolina, to be trained as a voter-education leader. At the end of the week-long workshop, she and five other friends, including a 16-year-old girl, Annelle Ponder, boarded a bus for the long trip back to Ruleville. At the bus station in Winona, Mississippi, she stayed on the bus while her friends got off to refresh themselves in the station. Some minutes later, policemen came out, dragging the women with them, and shoving them into police cars. Hamer hurried off the bus to see what was wrong, only to be shoved in a police car herself. All six women were under arrest, although when they arrived at the police station, the police were at a loss over what to charge them with. Finally, they settled on "disturbing the peace," although their real offense was daring to use a "whites only" restroom and ordering food in the bus station's eatery. They were all booked and jailed like criminals.

That night, Hamer sat in her jail cell and heard guards assaulting Ponder when she refused to say "Yes, Sir." The cops ripped off her clothes to the waist, beat her bloody, and punched her in the face so many times that it swelled. Hamer was next. A cop entered her cell, which she shared with a black prisoner, and ordered the man to beat her until she wished she were dead. The prisoner got up to do what he was told. Hamer turned to him and said, "'You mean you would do this to your own race?'" (Mills 1993: p. 60). He did not hesitate. As she lay on her stomach, he beat down on her so hard that for the rest of her short life she suffered from damaged kidneys.

Meanwhile SNCC workers knew something was wrong when the bus arrived in Ruleville without the women. After calling up all the police stations on the bus route, they finally located the women in the Winona jailhouse. It took the rest of the week to get them out of jail. The policemen in tiny Winona had never heard of SNCC and never would admit that they had violated anyone's human rights, but the phone calls made them refrain from beating the other women. Hamer bore no malice and actually smiled and exchanged greetings with her persecutors on the day of her release, to the surprise of everyone. She understood better than most what Dr. Martin Luther King, Jr., meant by *agape*—the unconditional, selfless love for others that has no expectations—a word she didn't know. Nevertheless, she practiced it in her heart.

The Justice Department in Washington, D.C. filed charges against the Winona policemen. Their trial took place in Oxford, Mississippi. Hamer was well enough to be present at the all-white jury's final verdict: not guilty. Hamer was not surprised; nor were other blacks. The verdict did not create a stir.

After that incident, Hamer told and retold the story of the beatings on her fundraising tours throughout the United States. She raised more money for SNCC than any other person. According to one SNCC officer, "'There were many strong leaders in Mississippi, but she was a cut above'" (Mills 1993: p. 7). She got to know Martin Luther King, Jr., and Andrew Young during the countless civil rights marches she participated in. In the meantime, the town of Winona, including the police department, was compelled to integrate.

As if 1963 hadn't been eventful enough, Fannie Lou Hamer decided to run for Congress that year. As she put it, "'We been waitin' all our lives and still gettin' killed, still gettin' hung, still gettin' beat to death. Now we're tired waitin'" (Mills 1993: p. 78). She lost out to her wealthy white opponent, but in 1964 ran for office again. She ran for the state senate in 1971. She lost these elections, but she felt the effort was worth it, even though death threats regularly accompanied her campaigns. "'If I fall,'" said the short, feisty Hamer, "'I'll fall five feet four inches forward in the fight for freedom'" (Mills 1993: p. 91). She was the first African American in the Mississippi Delta to run for political office in the 20th century.

Despite her failed campaigns, she set the stage, as no other grass-roots leader did in Mississippi, for other blacks to run for office in increasing numbers, especially, after the Voting Rights Act became law in 1965. And for the first time, white politicians were held accountable to their black citizens. This could be felt even in remote Sunflower County. For many years, the town council in Sunflower claimed that there wasn't enough money to provide the black neighborhood with adequate paving and street lighting. However, when the white mayor faced a popular black opponent during election year 1966, money miraculously appeared for improvements.

Fannie Lou Hamer became nationally known when she appeared on television at the Democratic National Convention in Atlantic City, New Jersey, in the summer of 1964. As a member of the black Mississippi Freedom Democratic Party (MFDP), she protested the official presence of the white delegation from Mississippi, a state that in practice denied the franchise to African Americans. She and her new party tried unsuccessfully to unseat the delegates. They succeeded four years later, at the 1968 Democratic National Convention in Chicago. On that occasion, Hamer received a thunderous standing ovation when she became the first African American to take her rightful seat as an official delegate at a national-party convention since the Reconstruction period after the Civil War, and the first woman ever from Mississippi.

Fannie Lou Hamer also led the fight to unseat her state's white male delegation in Congress. One of them, James Whitten, from Hamer's district, had been reelected in November 1964, on a day when 50 blacks had tried and failed to register to vote in the Indianola Courthouse. In the end, there were not enough votes during roll call in the House of Representatives to unseat the representatives, but a signal was sent to Congress. Seventy Congressmen stood up with Representative William Ryan, a Democrat from New York, on January 4, 1965, when he rose to challenge the Mississippi delegation's right to represent its state.

One of Hamer's great admirers was singer Harry Belafonte. Morale among SNCC workers in Mississippi was low after the 1964 Democratic Convention, and despite their most strenuous efforts, the number of black registered voters in the state was still small. The Civil Rights Act of 1964, which enforced desegregation in private and public establishments, accommodations, parks, and the like, did nothing to remove obstacles to voting, since it was still up to the states to set voting requirements.

Belafonte decided to take Hamer and a handful of other SNCC workers on a three-week trip with him to the African country of Guinea, whose ruler, Sékou Touré, was a personal friend of his. Hamer had never been abroad. The trip was like a shot of adrenaline to her and the other

SNCC workers. "'I had never in my life seen where black people were running banks . . . I had never seen nobody black running the government in my life'" (Mills 1993: p. 137). Not surprisingly, Hamer reported that "'I was treated much better in Africa than I ever was treated in America'" (Mills 1993: p. 135). When newspapers repeated this remark, many white Americans indignantly asked—if she didn't like America, then why didn't she just pack up and go back to Africa? Hamer was quick to retort that she'd go back to Africa when German Americans returned to Germany, Italian Americans to Italy, Irish Americans to Ireland, and so forth.

The visit to Africa gave her and her fellow SNCC workers hope for the future. Indeed, hope was just around the corner, in the form of the landmark Voting Rights Act, which President Lyndon B. Johnson signed on August 6, 1965. This federal law required states to eliminate all obstacles to voting, such as poll taxes and literacy tests.

One might think that civil rights activists could now pack their bags and leave Mississippi. But a law on paper did little good unless it was enforced. Klansmen still terrorized many blacks who had the courage to register to vote, and white policemen would do little to apprehend them. African Americans, despite their numbers, still lacked political and financial clout.

Fannie Lou Hamer turned her efforts increasingly to the welfare of disadvantaged blacks and whites. She even prophesied that the South would one day lead the nation in granting justice to all. Her views ran counter to SNCC's increasingly militant stance. She watched in dismay as the SNCC leadership began expelling whites, repudiating nonviolence in favor of militant black separatism, even criticizing her for being "irrelevant" and behind the times. While this hurt her very much, she spent the next 12 years until her death working for change, despite her increasing ill health, lack of medical insurance, and her husband's chronic unemployment.

In 1968, she started the "Pig Bank" to ensure that enough local families had meat on the table. The bank raised money to buy pigs and lend them out to families who bred them, while keeping some for themselves and giving away the rest to other families, who in turn did the same thing. In this way she put food on the table of nearly 300 families in and around Ruleville. In 1969, with generous funding from Harry Belafonte, Hamer started Freedom Farm Coop. Initially consisting of 40 acres, Coop members who paid a dollar a month (and many couldn't afford even that) planted and harvested food for themselves on the Coop's land. In 1971, the farm expanded to more than 640 acres. These relief efforts benefited both blacks and whites. Eventually, an organization of whites in Madison, Wisconsin called Measure for Measure raised much of the funds to keep Freedom Farm going. Soon the Coop was buying houses and renovating and selling them cheaply, so that poor people could become homeowners.

At the same time, Fannie Lou Hamer was the heart and soul of the voter-registration drive in her area, becoming the administrator for the Voter Education Project (VEP) grants. She helped attract a garment factory to the outskirts of Ruleville to provide employment opportunities to unemployed sharecroppers. And there were many. Handpicking cotton was finally dying out. Thousands began losing their jobs in the late 1960s. The textile factory and the day-care center she established, with the help of the National Council of Negro Women, helped many families through the hard times.

Despite all that Freedom Farm accomplished, poor weather, bad harvests, and overwhelming debts forced it to shut down in the fall of 1976. Fannie Lou Hamer's heart broke. At the same time, she was diagnosed with breast cancer and had no money to pay her medical bills. A kind doctor who knew of her work helped her to qualify for disability payments, which eventually covered her medical needs. Her heart gave out on March 14, 1977, after cancer treatments failed.

Her funeral was so large that a second church in Ruleville had to take care of the overflowing crowd of people. Rev. Andrew Young, by then a United Nations ambassador, arrived in a limousine to deliver the funeral oration. Other civil rights leaders carried her simple coffin to its grave. Ruleville had never seen anything like that day. A town that had scorned and tormented Hamer and her family had begun to honor her, even while she was alive, with a special Fannie Lou Hamer Day. The mourning at her passing was genuine.

Fannie Lou Hamer was not like the Mary Church Terrells, Martin Luther Kings and Thurgood Marshalls of this world, who grew up with some advantages, despite the fact of belonging to an oppressed group. She graduated from the school of hardship and poverty. She was born into the lowest rung of society and always lived in rural, depressed areas. Religion rather than books was her guiding light. With all her disadvantages, she became a hero and a leader. Because of her, many disadvantaged rural people, both black and white, gained the precious right to vote and make a better life for their children.

Chronology

OCTOBER 6, 1917	Fannie Lou Hamer is born in Montgomery County, Mississippi
1923	begins working in cotton fields
1944	marries sharecropper Perry Hamer and settles on Marlowe Plantation outside of Ruleville, Mississippi
AUGUST 26, 1962	attends first mass meeting on voter registration organized by SNCC and SCLC
AUGUST 31, 1962	is evicted from Marlowe Plantation after attempting to register to vote; begins working for SNCC
JANUARY 1963	becomes registered voter
JUNE 1963	is arrested and brutally beaten in jail in Winona, Mississippi, en route from voter education classes in Charleston, South Carolina
JUNE 1964	is defeated in bid to become Democratic candidate for Congress
AUGUST 1964	unsuccessfully challenges all-white Mississippi delegation at National Democratic Party Convention in Atlantic City, New Jersey
SEPTEMBER 1964	travels to Africa with Harry Belafonte and SNCC workers
NOVEMBER 1964	runs for Congress and loses

AUGUST 1968	is seated as official delegate at National Democratic Party Convention, Chicago
1968	creates Pig Bank to help needy families
1969	founds Freedom Farm
1971	runs unsuccessfully for Mississippi state senate seat
MARCH 14, 1977	Hamer dies of breast cancer outside of Ruleville, Mississippi

Further Reading

Books About Fannie Lou Hamer

Colman, Penny. *Fannie Lou Hamer & the Fight for the Vote.* Brookfield, Conn.: Millbrook Press, 1993. An engagingly written, brief story of Fannie Lou Hamer's life for the young reader, with many compelling photographs.

Kling, Susan. *Fannie Lou Hamer, A Biography.* Chicago: Women for Racial & Economic Equality, 1979. A short, 56-page summary of Fannie Lou Hamer's life and accomplishments, illustrated and very readable.

Mills, Kay. *This Little Light of Mine.* New York: Penguin Books, 1993. The only full-length, adult biography of the sharecropper turned civil rights activist, by a young journalist who traveled on her own to Mississippi to meet Hamer toward the end of her life.

Martin Luther King, Jr.

UNARMED REVOLUTIONARY
(1929–1968)

" The preacher's role was to keep hope alive in nearly hopeless situations," affirmed Coretta Scott King, the widow of the Reverend Martin Luther King, Jr., (C. S. King 1993: p. 29). All black ministers instilled in their congregations a sense that they were God's beloved. But some went a step further and worked for justice on behalf of African Americans. Martin Luther King, Jr., was one of them. Moreover, he incorporated Mahatma Gandhi's spiritual principles of nonviolence into his Christian framework. As King matured, he became a political and spiritual leader—a black Moses who would lead his people to freedom.

☆　☆　☆

On January 15, 1929, Martin Luther King, Jr., was born into a Southern middle-class family. He grew up in a lovely, graceful house in a white neighborhood in segregated Georgia. His life was unusually privileged, just the opposite of that of his father, the self-made businessman and assistant pastor of Ebenezer Baptist Church. King's mother Alberta was a preacher's daughter and a college graduate, the latter a rarity among African-American women at the time. Besides Martin, the Kings had one daughter, Christine, and another son, Alfred Daniel, who also became a minister.

As an adult, when he was already marked as a great leader, Martin Luther King, Jr., said that loving came easily to him because he had known only love and family harmony while growing up. But even the sheltered, much loved boy inevitably felt the sting of racism. One of his most painful experiences occurred shortly after he had started first grade in the segregated elementary school. Up until then, he was used to playing with the white children in his neighborhood, and he had a best friend who was white. One day his pals refused to play with him "'because we're white and you're colored'" (C. S. King 1993: p. 79). He ran home in tears. His grandmother, who doted on him, took him on her lap and explained to him for the first time the history of slavery and African-American suffering since the Civil War. She cautioned him never to hate whites, however, but to pray for them instead.

King's father, Pastor King (nicknamed Daddy King), was an activist minister and even practiced his own form of resistance to racial discrimination. On the day he registered to vote, he defiantly rode up the "whites only" elevator to the voter-registration booth; he founded the Atlanta branch of the NAACP, and he won the fight for equal pay for black teachers in Atlanta.

Daddy King's example rubbed off on his son. When he was only 15, young King took a summer job in Atlanta as a laborer, even though his father could have found him a much better job. What he learned firsthand was how oppressive conditions were for so many poor, underpaid black workers, whose white bosses spoke to them demeaningly and hurled racial slurs at them. The following summer, King and a group of his high school friends went to work as farm

Opposite: The Reverend Martin Luther King, Jr., his wife Coretta Scott, and three of their four children: daughter Yolanda and sons Dexter and Martin Luther King III. (National Archives)

MARTIN LUTHER KING, JR.

laborers in Connecticut, in part to experience for themselves how Northerners treated African Americans. A surprised King wrote to his parents that at the end of the work day, they could enter any restaurant in town and be served courteously. His resentment deepened at the South's blatant discrimination against African Americans.

King was not always a serious youngster. In fact, he never bothered studying much in high school, because he was having too much fun. He scraped by, semester after semester, with a C average. Because of his high intelligence, he was still able to pass the entrance exam to prestigious Morehouse College in Atlanta, even though he was not very studious. Morehouse was a black college founded by white Baptists after the Civil War. King's father was a graduate and a trustee of the college.

At first young King resisted following his father into the ministry. Young as he was, he was uncomfortable with the blind, simple faith so common at Ebenezer Baptist Church, as well as with his father's rigid fundamentalism. However, when his friends asked him to lead group evening prayers during their summer in Connecticut, King felt the first stirrings of a religious calling. As a college student he came under the influence of exceptional men, such as the college president, Dr. Benjamin E. Mays, and Professor George D. Kelsey, who were up-to-date intellectuals as well as ordained ministers. Finally, at age 18, King made his father happy when he asked to be ordained. This was a relatively simple matter in the Baptist church and required no formal seminary training. King's father ordained his son, right in their church. The new minister's sermon that Sunday deeply stirred the congregation, and he began to show signs of the charisma that is the mark of a natural leader.

Remaining an untrained minister, however, was far from young King's intentions. He was only 19 when he graduated from Morehouse in three years, by virtue of his heavy course loads. His grades had been good but not excellent; nonetheless, strong letters of recommendation secured his acceptance into Crozer Theological Seminary, a Baptist school outside of Philadelphia. For the first time, King would study with a white majority, a new experience for him.

At Crozer, King finally began earning As in most of his subjects. From time to time, professors wrote personal assessments of their students. King struck his professors as an individualist who disliked team work, who seemed too stuck up and arrogant to be an effective minister. Otherwise, they had nothing but praise for his intellectual gifts.

As a student at Crozer, Martin became attracted to Mohandas Gandhi's philosophy of nonviolent resistance. Gandhi was an Indian civil rights leader who is credited with leading his nation to throw off British rule in the 1940s. One day King went to a Philadelphia bookstore and bought every book on Gandhi that he could find. However, it would take years for him to integrate Gandhian thought and strategy into his own theology.

A proud family photograph portrays King standing in his graduation gown at Crozer in 1951: a young man of medium height, stocky, and with a face remarkable for its sweetness of expression. King's family was delighted that he had graduated at the top of his class. He seemed destined for a brilliant career as a doctoral student of theology at Boston University (BU).

King's decision to pursue his Ph.D., the highest academic degree, put him in a tiny minority among black Baptist ministers. Only 10 percent of black ministers had any seminary training at all. King's own father had none. At BU, Martin studied with some of the most eminent theologians in America. By then he could read Latin, Greek, and Hebrew, and he was drawn to an in-depth study of the personality of God. He believed that God was more than the source of all good, that God had a distinct personality and took an active role in the life of humankind. This was the philosophy of personalism, whose main exponent, Professor Edgar S. Brightman, became King's mentor at school.

While a student at BU, King would often preach at black churches in and around the city. His sermons always seemed to inspire and touch the lives of all his listeners. One day a friend of his, Mary Powell, told her friend Coretta Scott about the gifted preacher, hoping that she would want to meet him. At the time, Scott was an advanced student at the Boston Conservatory of Music and had plans to become an opera singer. "The moment Mary told me the young man was a minister, I lost interest," Scott recalled (C. S. King 1993: p. 50). She disliked the "overly pious" type.

She did meet him, however, in 1952. For King it was love at first sight, though not for Scott. Ultimately, what won her over was the undeniable fact that "He was good—such a very good man'" (C. S. King 1993: p. 59). After a courtship that lasted 18 months, they married in her parents' home in Alabama on June 18, 1953. Afterward they returned to complete their studies in Boston, where they rented a small apartment and took turns cooking, cleaning, and doing laundry.

They celebrated Coretta's graduation from the Boston Conservatory of Music in 1954 by visiting an amusement park, to his mother-in-law's surprise. "Martin rode all the rides, and he and Philip Lenud roller-skated until they were ready to drop, laughing and roughhousing and doing fancy turns and gyrations" (C. S. King 1993: p. 89). King believed humor and fun and God were not mutually exclusive.

King now accepted the pastorship of Dexter Avenue Baptist Church in Montgomery, Alabama, and he finished writing his dissertation (a book-length, original research paper required for a Ph.D.) a year later. Coretta had grown up on a farm 80 miles away and had spent most of her life trying to get away from the South. Leaving behind her beloved Boston and a glamorous singing career were the first of her many painful sacrifices. For his part, King could have chosen to stay in Boston, which he liked and where he could have lived a comfortable life. But before they married, he had told Coretta, "'I'm going to live in the South because that's where I'm needed'" (C. S. King 1993: p. 90). She accepted that choice, and the Kings returned to the South.

Dexter Avenue Baptist Church was a snug brick building situated on Montgomery's historic downtown square. King was determined to be an activist minister from the start. He urged everyone in his congregation to join the NAACP, and he spearheaded a voter-registration drive. Other preachers in Montgomery, who were much less educated than King, began to look up to the young Baptist minister.

Church members loved their dedicated pastor and his glamorous wife. In the spring of 1955, their comfortable home was filled with the happy gurgling of their first baby, Yolanda. Two boys, Dexter and Martin Luther King III, and one more girl, Bernice, were born in subsequent years.

The day arrived when the Kings learned of Rosa Parks' courageous refusal to yield her bus seat to a white man. The very next day, December 2, 1955, King threw open his church's doors for a public meeting. In the cadences and rhythms of traditional Baptist preachers, he called on men and women to reject evil: "'He who accepts evil without protesting against it is really cooperating with it'" (C. S. King 1993: p. 109). He liked to quote Booker T. Washington, saying, "'Let no man pull you so low as to make you hate him'" (C. S. King 1993: p. 109). Love your enemy, King always exhorted, paraphrasing some of the best-known words from the New Testament. The Bible's admonition to love one's enemy sounded simple, but in fact, King hadn't really understood those words until he began studying Greek in seminary. In one of his Sunday sermons, he explained that in Greek, there were different words for love, in contrast to the single word in English. Thus, *eros* referred to romantic love; *phila* was the word for the fond, affectionate, love that one feels for family and friends. These kinds of love, King explained, were impossible to have for one's oppressor. But *agape*—an active unselfish love desiring the good of another without expecting anything in return—was not only possible but imperative.

Agape became the guiding principle in the long and strenuous Montgomery bus boycott, in the course of which white supremacists firebombed King's home, as well as those of other boycott leaders. King and dozens of other ministers suffered arrest. But during the whole 381-day ordeal, when all odds seemed to be on the side of the oppressors, the preachers kept hope alive. At the outset of the boycott, they had asked King to head the Montgomery Improvement Association (MIA). In this position, the gentle preacher turned into the boycott's field commander and its chief negotiator with the stubborn and staunchly racist Montgomery city government. Hope finally paid off when the Supreme Court ruled that segregated busing was illegal in November 1956. By then the young Martin Luther King, Jr., was a famous man.

What to do now that the boycott was over was the question he pondered while writing his first book, *Stride Toward Freedom: The*

Montgomery Story, published in 1958. He decided to ask his fellow church leaders. He invited 100 African-American ministers in the South to a meeting in his father's church in Atlanta to discuss the possibility of ending segregation, once and for all.

In February 1957, the Southern Christian Leadership Conference (SCLC) came into being. From then on, the SCLC led by King would direct the black liberation struggle. The Montgomery bus boycott had taught them all how arduous this task would be.

A month later, King and his wife received an invitation to attend the independence day celebrations in Ghana, Africa, which had newly liberated itself from British colonial rule. For a long time, King had felt there was a connection between the freedom struggle at home and black liberation from white colonial rule in Africa. Traveling with King and his wife was A. Philip Randolph, the old civil-rights warrior. From Ghana they all visited Nigeria, and everywhere they went they felt the pulse of black freedom and rebirth. The Kings traveled on to Europe, which they had never seen. Rome particularly impressed them, a city that seemed to symbolize man's abiding relationship with God. When he entered St. Peter's Basilica, Martin Luther King, Jr., a lifelong Southern Baptist, was so overwhelmed by the church's spiritual power that he fell on his knees and prayed.

Returning to the United States in late spring of 1958, King was in great demand as a speaker. On a promotional tour of his first book in September, which would help raise money for the movement, King found himself in a Harlem bookstore. Suddenly, a deranged African-American woman plunged a knife deep into his chest. King remained conscious in the ensuing chaos. The knife was so close to his heart that, as he found out later, the smallest cough would have killed him.

After serious surgery and months of recovery, King was finally discharged from the hospital. A few days later, in March 1959, he was on his way with Coretta to India. The homeland of the revered Mohandas Gandhi, "the father of the Indian nation," had invited them as honored guests.

No journey in King's life ever meant more to him. To meet with Gandhi's disciples, to lay eyes on the places where the Indian leader had lived, worshipped, and led his movement turned into a spiritual odyssey for the young pastor. From then on, Coretta King recalled, her husband lost all interest in material things, including his own appearance; nothing mattered to him anymore except the good of others, especially the welfare of the oppressed. While he loved his wife and four children, they saw less and less of him. Soon he was away from home three weeks out of every four.

"Christ furnished the spirit, Gandhi showed how it would work," became King's motto (C. S. King 1993: p. 56). Gandhi taught that if the goal was righteous, then the means to that goal must be moral in the sight of God. There was nothing wrong with force or confrontation, as long as it was nonviolent and without hatred of the oppressor.

The next five years, beginning in early 1960 with the student sit-ins, were the most hectic in King's life. During this period, students would sit at a segregated lunch counter or table and refuse to leave until the owner desegregated the restaurant. Usually the owner called the police, who would arrest the students. King himself would be arrested over and over again, kicked and spat at, cursed, and threatened. As if that were not enough, the FBI, headed by J. Edgar Hoover, had King's phones illegally tapped and spread rumors that King was unfaithful to his wife and had pro-Communist sympathies. Almost as bad was disaffection in his own movement: the Student Non-Violent Coordinating Committee (SNCC) which the Student Christian Leadership Conference (SCLC) established in 1960, criticized King as weak and slow to act. SNCC eventually abandoned King's nonviolent creed. The NAACP, too, was always wary of King, preferring litigation in the courts over mass protest. The SCLC and its core leadership, however, remained loyal to King.

When King returned home from India he knew he could no longer give himself wholly to Dexter Avenue Baptist Church. To the dismay of his congregants, he resigned. The family bade the church a tearful farewell and headed for Atlanta, where King accepted Ebenezer's offer to become co-pastor of their church. The Kings' first son, however, was named Dexter in honor of his father's first ministry.

King and his closest companion, Rev. Ralph Abernathy, provided moral support to the many SNCC sit-ins in 1960, aiming to desegregate lunch counters and restaurants throughout the South. Along with SNCC leaders, they often suffered arrest. In early 1961, the

Congress for Racial Equality (CORE) under the leadership of James Farmer began organizing "freedom rides," busloads of Northern civil rights activists who boarded Greyhounds headed for segregated bus terminals in the South. Violence often greeted the riders when they arrived. In May 1961, King spent the entire night with 1,200 freedom riders in Ralph Abernathy's church in Montgomery as an angry white mob surrounded the church, threatening to burn it to the ground. Only the timely arrival of federal marshalls subdued the violent crowd. Perhaps because of all the media attention this incident received, the federal Interstate Commerce Commission outlawed segregation on interstate travel on November 1, 1963.

John F. Kennedy (JFK), the charismatic young president, dragged his heels in initiating civil-rights legislation in Congress because he was afraid to antagonize Southern legislators. After meeting with JFK in the White House in January of 1963, King, Abernathy, and other SCLC leaders left empty-handed.

King believed the SCLC should force a showdown with the government, much as A. Philip Randolph had done in 1941 when he threatened to march thousands of African Americans past the White House. Birmingham, Alabama, rather than Washington, D.C., would be SCLC's target. Birmingham was chosen because, said King, "'All the evils and injustices the Negro can be subjected to are right there in Birmingham'" (C. S. King 1993: p. 201). Moreover, Rev. Fred L. Shuttlesworth, leader of the Alabama Christian Movement for Human Rights, was a member of SCLC. Shuttlesworth's campaign to desegregate Birmingham was getting nowhere. But King's arrival in town on April 13, 1963 changed that.

King's presence instantly set off alarm bells in most white churches, whose religious leaders opposed the "invasion" of their city by "extremists." The white-controlled city government had managed to get a court order prohibiting public demonstrations. Police arrested King and Abernathy for defying the injunction and threw them into solitary confinement for eight days.

Using scraps of old newspaper, even toilet paper, King wrote his famous "Letter from Birmingham Jail," considered among his finest writing. It was directed at the white clergymen opposing the "extremist" SCLC's presence in Birmingham. "'Was not Jesus an extremist for love?'" King asked. Were not his Apostles extremists? "'I am in Birmingham because injustice is here'" (C. S. King 1993: p. 212). From then on, his "letter" became the touchstone of the civil rights movement.

Released from jail on April 20, King attended a strategy meeting, the upshot of which was the daring decision to recruit local school-children to march in the streets for freedom. Rev. Andrew Young was in charge of recruiting and training the volunteer children in non-violent tactics. When the day arrived for them to march, May 2, police arrested more than 900 of the peaceful, excited children. The next day, 1,000 more appeared. The jails couldn't contain them all. This time the commissioner of public safety, the racist Eugene ("Bull") Connor, instructed police to turn the fire hoses on the demonstrators to force them to disperse. "'Jets of water under 100 pounds of pressure knocked the children flat, ripping the clothes off some of them. Then Connor unleashed the police dogs—they ran wild, biting the children'" (C. S. King 1993: p. 213). All of this was broadcast live on television to a worldwide audience. As a result, countless Americans were won over to the civil rights struggle. Many wrote, telegrammed and telephoned Congress and the White House to support the demonstrators.

At last, the city government had had enough and sat down to negotiate with King. The result was the complete acceptance of all the SCLC's demands. "'Bull Connor has done as much for civil rights as Abraham Lincoln'" (C. S. King 1993: p. 217), joked President Kennedy, who felt the time was now ripe to send a landmark civil rights bill to Congress.

Despite the ugly incidents that were the price of the SCLC's great victory (King's brother's house in Birmingham was firebombed, as well as a black church two months later, which resulted in the deaths of four small girls), Gandhi's tactics of nonviolent confrontation clearly seemed to work. At one point, police in Birmingham refused to follow orders to once again set the hoses on praying demonstrators, "'the first crack in the morale of the racist forces,'" according to Coretta King, who was present at the event (C. S. King 1993: p. 214). Moreover, thousands of cities throughout the South voluntarily desegregated in the following weeks and months. There was also a civil-rights bill pending in Congress that would outlaw segregation in public and private eating establishments, parks, hotels, and the like.

Two months later, Washington, D.C. was brimming over with 250,000 black and white demonstrators, who came to rally on behalf of civil rights at the Lincoln Memorial. August 28 dawned hot and sticky; hundreds of thousands of hands applauded speech after speech, and voices cheered when Mahalia Jackson finished singing. King, who had stayed up all night preparing his speech, was nervous that the crowd's interest would wane when he, the last speaker of the day, walked to the podium to deliver his address.

The restless audience grew noticeably quiet as they heard his familiar voice. "'America has given the Negro a bad check. We are here today to redeem that check. I will not accept the idea that there is no money in the Bank of Justice'" (C. S. King 1993: p. 222). That was only part of the speech he had written the night before; King stopped looking at his notes and began speaking words from his heart. When he concluded with his majestic exclamation, "Free at last! Free at last! Great God A-mighty, we are free at last!" there was complete silence. A minute later, the greatest thunder of applause that Washington, D.C. had ever heard broke out. By then King was whisked away for a meeting with the president, who had been watching everything on his TV in the Oval Office. Never before was King's prestige and moral stature higher than on that day, except, perhaps, when he received the Nobel Peace Prize in the following year, the first African American (and the youngest person) to receive that high honor.

Despite all this, King had enemies, but none more powerful than the director of the FBI, J. Edgar Hoover. Even presidents feared Hoover, who had information on everybody in power or with influence. And Hoover had conceived an intense, irrational hatred for King. FBI agents followed King everywhere and illegally tapped his phone at work and at home. Hoover tried to convince Kennedy and, later, President Johnson that King was not only a Communist, but according to Hoover, an adulterer. Hoover hoped King's wife would divorce him. In this way he also sought to damage King's reputation.

King at the Berlin Wall in September 1964, with devoted partner and friend, Rev. Ralph Abernathy, half-hidden beside him. (National Archives)

Certainly no one in the civil rights movement, even those who had no love for King, ever produced evidence of marital infidelities, though it was widely known that many women were attracted to the eloquent preacher. In all the years since his death, no woman has ever come forward to claim that she had an illicit relationship with him. Coretta King refused to believe the rumors. The FBI investigation of King in the long run got nowhere, while Hoover's wide-ranging illegal activities were brought to light after his death in 1972.

The civil rights bill, which Kennedy sponsored, did not become law until 1964, largely because of the disruption following the president's assassination only three months after the March on Washington. When King learned of the president's murder, he turned to his wife, and with resignation in his voice he remarked,

"'This is what is going to happen to me also'" (C. S. King 1993: p. 227).

The new Civil Rights Act banned discrimination in housing, employment, and public accommodations and established the Equal Employment Opportunity Commission to investigate claims of bias. But the final passage of the Civil Rights Act of 1964 did not deter the SCLC from launching a major drive for black voter registration throughout the South. Civil rights might be guaranteed on paper, but the new law did not remove obstructions to voting, such as the poll tax and literacy tests. SNCC volunteers, black and white, entered thousands of communities to organize voter-registration drives, especially in Alabama, where registration obstruction was at its worst.

In early 1965, King targeted Selma, the heart of black, rural Alabama, where 99 percent of the registered voters were white. He arrived there in mid-January. A white supremacist, who had been trailing him everywhere, brutally assaulted him in broad daylight, but King was not seriously hurt. In the ensuing weeks, a local black man was beaten to death in a demonstration, and police arrested King and Abernathy for leading an unauthorized march to the Selma Courthouse and threw them into solitary confinement. The fiery black nationalist Malcolm X visited King in jail. King greeted him with brotherly affection, but they remained poles apart in their philosophies. At this time, Malcolm X rejected nonviolence and preached "an eye for an eye and a tooth for a tooth" instead. He also initially believed that blacks should separate themselves from whites and reject integration. After King got out of jail, he flew to Washington to alert President Johnson about the hardships SNCC volunteers faced in their attempts to register voters. When he returned, he announced a 54-mile pedestrian crusade to press for voting rights that would begin in Selma and end in Alabama's capital, Montgomery. King made a public appeal to clergymen and women of all faiths to join the demonstrators in Selma. Soon, a group of Roman Catholic nuns appeared, as well as priests and rabbis. Half the demonstrators by then were white. What followed on March 20, 1965 (after the injunction against demonstrating had been rescinded) was a courageous and terrifying two-day march of 5,000 people to Montgomery. All along the route, white supremacists gathered to heckle and harass the marchers. President Johnson was moved to send his voting-rights bill to Congress. Until it became law, nothing would change in Alabama. After eloquent speeches in front of Montgomery's Capitol, the demonstration dispersed.

On August 6, 1965, several months after the Selma march, the Voting Rights Act became law. Any obstruction to voting henceforth became a punishable crime. Discrimination on the basis of race was illegal everywhere, and voting rights were secure. King could afford to rest on his laurels and spend time with his neglected family and church.

But it was hard to stop after 10 years of crusading. In January 1967, he finally took an extended vacation with his family, traveling to Jamaica, where he spent a good deal of time writing his second book, *Where Do We Go From Here: Chaos or Community?*, a commentary on the past and present civil rights movements. On his return to the States, it was clear to King that there were still many mountains to climb, many injustices to rectify. With segregation at an end in the South, King announced to the SCLC his intention to assault racism in the North.

This was an unpopular move; for one, Northern whites had lent King crucial support—both financial and moral—throughout his campaign. For another, racism in the North was far less clearly defined than in the South and would be far more difficult to combat. In Chicago, his first target, he encountered no brutal police nor recalcitrant city government. Yet moving his family in 1966 into a Chicago slum to bring attention to the plight of slum dwellers antagonized many and led to rioting in Chicago's poor Southside. His "Poor People's Campaign" in the late 1960s did create soup kitchens and homeless shelters, but it failed to create improvements in the lives of blacks, Hispanics, and other minorities that he had hoped for.

Many Americans, including his followers, were antagonized by King's increasingly vocal criticism of the Vietnam War. In the spring of 1967, for the first time in his life, he led an antiwar march through the heart of New York City; soon afterward, he was calling on both black and white men of draft age to become conscientious objectors (someone who refuses to be drafted into the military because it violates that person's conscience). To King, the war was utterly senseless. "'It is estimated,'" he said in one speech, "'that we spend $322,000 for each enemy we kill, while we spend . . . in America only $53 for each person classified as poor'" (C. S. King 1993: p. 272).

Nonetheless, even Andrew Young criticized King for moving away from the most pressing issue of all, black poverty. Black leaders, such as Whitney Young of the Urban League and Ralph Bunche of the United Nations, feared that President Johnson, who had done so much for civil rights, would pay less attention to the plight of African Americans because of King's antiwar stance. White newspapers and magazines, hitherto so supportive, now sharply criticized King, to his great personal pain. In 1967 and even as late as 1968 (although this would change by the end of the year) most of the country still supported the war.

In the meantime, in 1968 sanitation workers in Memphis were getting nowhere in their strike against the city's sanitation department. The workers were all African American and for years they had put up with the worst pay in the city. Finally, the Sanitation Workers Union turned to King for moral support. King, Rev. Jesse Jackson, Andrew Young, and Hosea Williams arrived in Memphis in the beginning of April. That night, King delivered an unusually prophetic speech. "'Like anybody else, I would like to live a long life. Longevity has its place. But I'm not concerned about that now. I just want to do God's will. And he's allowed me to go up to the mountain. And I've looked over, and I've seen the Promised Land'" (C. S. King 1993: p. 291). The next day, April 4, King was standing on the balcony of his motel along with his closest aides. It was late afternoon. A white racist, James Earl Ray, wielding an assault weapon, shot and mortally wounded King. He never regained consciousness and died in the hospital a few hours later. Easter was around the corner. "'It was somewhat strange, yet reassuring, that his death would come so close to the anniversary of the death of his Lord and Master'" wrote his widow (C. S. King 1993: pp. 295–296).

King had compressed many lifetimes into his short life. In 1985, Congress declared his birthday a national holiday, but even so, not every state has chosen to honor King in this way. By adopting this holiday, the nation recognizes that because of King, America has become a better country. Martin Luther King, Jr., a religious leader first and foremost, had helped his country regain some of the moral ground it had lost during the many years in which the civil and human rights of blacks were violated while those in power looked the other way.

Chronology

JANUARY 15, 1929	Martin Luther King, Jr., born in Atlanta, Georgia
1947	ordained as assistant pastor in Ebenezer Baptist Church
1948	graduates from Morehouse College
1951	graduates from Crozer Theological Seminary
1953	marries Coretta Scott, opera singer
1955	graduates with doctorate in theology from Boston University
1955	serves as president of Montgomery Improvement Association (MIA); leads bus boycott
1957	founds Southern Christian Leadership Conference (SCLC)
1958	first book published; stabbed and seriously wounded by deranged woman in Harlem
1959	King travels to India
1963	inaugurates Birmingham campaign; writes famous "Letter from Birmingham Jail"; March on Washington, D.C., where he delivers "I Have a Dream" speech
1964	King receives Nobel Peace Prize
1965	inaugurates Selma campaign

1966	inaugurates Chicago campaign
1967	second book published
1967–1968	King plans Poor People's campaign
APRIL 4, 1968	Assassinated in Memphis, Tennessee
1985	King's birthday declared a national holiday

Further Reading

By Martin Luther King, Jr.

King, Jr., Martin Luther. *Stride Toward Freedom: the Montgomery Story.* New York: Harper, 1958. A graphic, firsthand account of the Montgomery bus boycott and its long range significance.

———. *Where Do We Go From Here: Chaos or Community?* New York: Harper & Row, 1967. Reflections on the civil rights movement, its achievements, and future goals.

About Martin Luther King, Jr.

Haskins, James. *The Day Martin Luther King, Jr. Was Shot: A Photo History of the Civil Rights Movement.* New York: Scholastic, Inc., 1992. This 100-page book includes brief text, lots of photos, as well as bibliography for young readers.

———. *The Life & Death of Martin Luther King, Jr.* New York: Beech Tree Books, 1992. A concise biography, richly illustrated, that also tries to answer questions surrounding King's assassination.

King, Coretta Scott. *My Life With Martin Luther King, Jr.*, revised edition. New York: Henry Holt & Co., 1993. Coretta Scott King's recollections of her life with her late husband, simply and effectively told.

King, Martin Luther, Sr. *Daddy King: An Autobiography.* New York: Morrow, 1980. Very personal account of the life of the person who most influenced King, Jr.

Index

Boldface numbers indicate main topics. *Italic* page numbers indicate illustrations or captions.